Faith-Based Huma

2018 Edition

By David A. Robinson

Contents

This page is intentionally blank.

Introduction

When I was a child in the early 1960s, there was a kids' program on Channel 3 TV in Hartford, Connecticut (then WTIC-TV, now WFSB-TV) called "The Ranger Andy Show." It aired every weekday at 4:00 pm after school. I and thousands of other Connecticut and western Massachusetts kids watched that show religiously. When I say "religiously," I mean it figuratively but also somewhat literally. Once a week, Ranger Andy would take out his banjo and sing a song called "You'll Find It in the Bible." He would find biblical guidance for virtually all of life's problems in that song. Many of us would listen to that song and, when we needed answers to life's problems, try to "find it in the Bible." Indeed, until 1963 most public schools, including the ones I attended, began the day by leading the students to recite the Lord's Prayer (Matthew 6:9-13).

Times have changed. Since 1963, public schools in the United States have been prohibited from leading students in daily prayer. I don't watch children's TV anymore, but my guess is that the Bible is rarely, if ever, mentioned in children's programming on regular (non-religious) weekday TV these days in Connecticut. I don't know about other parts of the country. According to a recent Gallup poll, Connecticut is one of the 10 least religious of the 50 states.

Nevertheless, many people, even in Connecticut, still want religion in their lives. This book discusses some Judeo-Christian teachings that apply to managing employees. It is for employers who, occasionally or often, think about God and the Bible when managing employees. It is primarily a book about law, business, and management, not about religion. But it has a religious flavor. The laws against discrimination in the workplace are based on biblical principles, as I will discuss. Most of this book focuses on how to prevent discrimination in the workplace, but the book also touches on broader HR issues such as wages and profits.

After 40 years of advising employers about labor law, employment law, and human resource management, I have arrived at the following conclusion: For most employers, the best guide to earning a profit and complying with the law is to follow some biblical sayings. Of course, you may choose to follow (live by) all or many biblical sayings, not just some biblical sayings. That is for you to decide. I am a lawyer, not a preacher. In this book, I focus on the biblical sayings I think are most likely, if employers will follow them, to help employers earn a profit, comply with the law, provide better working conditions to employees, and feel good about it. There is no guarantee that you will achieve all these goals, even if you follow the Bible. But I think most (not all, but most) employers can increase their chance of success if they follow the biblical sayings I discuss in this book.

This book uses the word "manager" to refer to any employer: any executive, owner, manager, or supervisor of a business, nonprofit organization, or government entity.

This book does not try to make managers more religious. It does not try to convert anyone from one religion to another. It is for managers who enjoy reading the Bible (or reading passages from the Bible) and want to integrate the Bible into their managerial thinking. It provides them some guidance. Not all managers want to read the Bible. Not all managers want to integrate the Bible into their managerial thinking. Many managers are of other faiths. Some managers are atheists. Some managers do not want to hear about religion at all. That is OK. This book is not for every manager. It is for managers who want such a book.

You might expect a faith-based guide to human resource management to be a touchy-feely, warm-and-fuzzy pontification that favors employees over employers. This guide is not. This guide comes close to "worshipping" employers. Employers provide jobs. The Golden Rule—"Do unto others as you would have them do unto you" (Matthew 7:12)—is important but so is what Paul told the Corinthians: "He who sows sparingly will also reap sparingly, and he who sows bountifully will also reap bountifully" (2 Corinthians 9:6). In my opinion, those two biblical passages, together, mean this: Employees should be hired, compensated, promoted, disciplined, and terminated based on what their productivity and services are worth, not on their race, color, national origin, sex, age, religion, disability, sexual orientation, or other irrelevant or illegally discriminatory factor. By "worth," I mean worth to the employer. I wish I could mean "worth" in the eyes of God. In the eyes of God, a little-known employee who works hard and is paid the minimum wage is worth as much, if not more, than the famous ballplayer who is paid $20 million per year. But the $20 million per year ballplayer probably generates much more revenue (ticket sales, broadcast and cable TV revenues, T-shirts, etc.) for his employer than the minimum-wage employee does for his (the minimum-wage employee's) employer. Unless you are employed by God, you cannot expect your pay to be much more than your economic worth to your employer. According to the Bible, it is possible for an employer to earn a good profit with a clear conscience.

"You" and "Your"

It is employers, more so than employees, who are required to comply with the discrimination laws. So when this book refers to "you" or "your," it generally means employers. However, employees can also benefit from following the advice. Furthermore, an executive, supervisor, or other manager can be simultaneously an employer and an employee.

Disclaimer

The rights of employers and employees depend in part on which of the 50 states they are in, how many employees the employer has, whether the employer is public-sector or private-sector, and some other factors. There are, to be sure, federal employment laws—which are the same in every state—but there are also state employment laws. Some state laws provide greater protection to employees than the federal laws do. Some employers may be too small (small number of employees) to be governed by a federal law but large enough to be governed by a state law. So, there may be exceptions to some of the information contained in this book, depending on such factors. If you want legal advice about a particular situation, consult a lawyer in your state. Don't rely solely on this book. I am a lawyer licensed to practice law in Connecticut. I practiced law in Massachusetts for 31 years (1977-2008), then retired in Massachusetts after I moved to Connecticut. I have never practiced law in the other 48 states. This book is not "legal advice" and is not a substitute for legal advice.

Chapter 1

Employment, Law, and the Bible

In the United States, most employees, including the vast majority of employees who are not in unions and don't have contracts to work for a specific duration (for example, a three-year contract), are employees "at will." They can quit their job at any time for any reason or no reason. Their employer can terminate them at any time for any reason or no reason, except the employer cannot terminate them for an illegal reason. That is, the employer cannot terminate them if the employer's motivation for terminating them is the employee's race, sex, age, religion, disability, genetics, or some other factors. As examples of these other factors, the employer cannot terminate the employee if the employer's motivation for doing so is that the employee tried to organize a union, tried to collect overtime pay the employee reasonably believes he is entitled to, or "blew the whistle" on certain illegal activities of the employer. In Connecticut and at least 20 other states, an employer cannot terminate an employee for being gay or lesbian. There are some additional illegal reasons for terminating an employee, but I don't have space to list them all in this short book.

When an employer's motivation for terminating or penalizing an employee is any of those factors, it is called "discrimination." This book will discuss many (not all) types of employment discrimination.

Some people think employment "at will" is unfair to employees. They think it is unfair that the employer can terminate the employee at any time for any reason (except an illegal reason), or even for no reason. Sometimes it is unfair, but the alternative, in my opinion, is worse. The alternative is a law that says the employer can terminate an employee only for "just cause." An employer would be stuck with an employee for life unless the employee quits or the employer can prove the employee did something bad enough to justify termination. Employers would be afraid to hire anyone. Employers, especially small employers, do not want to be stuck with an employee for life. Union contracts, which are often 2-year or 3-year contracts, usually prohibit an employer to terminate an employee except for "just cause," as do some laws pertaining to government employees. As to most private-sector, nonunion employees in most states, the employer does not need "just cause" to terminate the employee. Employment "at will" is consistent with a free nation. An employee is not a slave. He is not required to work for the same company his whole life. Likewise, the same company is not required to employ him his whole life.

If you look at a dictionary, the word "discriminate," in and of itself, does not necessarily mean something bad or illegal. If someone has "discriminating taste," that is usually good, not bad. Some types of discrimination are legal. For example, you usually can discriminate in favor of employees whose job performance is good. You usually can discriminate against employees whose job performance is bad. But some types of discrimination—such as discrimination based on race, sex, age, religion, disability, or genetics—are illegal. Those classifications are often called "protected classifications." Sexual orientation discrimination is illegal ("protected classification") in some parts of the United States. Whether it is illegal in other parts of the United States will be discussed in chapter 8 (Prevent Sexual Orientation Discrimination).

There are some procedural strategies that many lawyers advise employers to use to prevent or reduce the likelihood of a lawsuit filed by an employee against the employer. One strategy is documentation of the employee's poor job performance (the "paper trail"). Other strategies include warnings, progressive discipline, employment-at-will statements, severance agreements in which the employee releases his right to sue, employment practices liability insurance, and perhaps some other strategies. I agree with many of these strategies, but I do not have space in this short book to discuss them. Furthermore, my advice about procedural strategies will often depend on the size, type, location (Connecticut, Massachusetts, or other state) and other particular circumstances of the employer, and therefore it is difficult to generalize about such strategies in a short book such as this. Talk to a lawyer to ascertain what the best strategy is for your particular company or organization.

One strategy for preventing or reducing the likelihood of an employment discrimination lawsuit—and this book focuses on this strategy—is to prevent discrimination in the first place. This book teaches employers how to prevent some of the more common types of illegal discrimination in the workplace and thereby, hopefully, prevent or reduce the impact or likelihood of a discrimination lawsuit. I'll discuss a few additional strategies in chapter 10 (Some Tips to Reduce Damages and Lawyers' Fees).

The Bible forbids or discourages the types of discrimination discussed in this book. But the Bible also forbids or discourages lawsuits. "Do not sue the Brethren . . . . It is already an utter failure for you that you go to law against one another," St. Paul said (1 Corinthians 6:1-7). "Avoid foolish disputes, genealogies, contentions, and strivings about the law; for they are unprofitable and useless," he said (Titus 3:9). Jesus suggested that if someone does us wrong, we should "turn the other cheek" rather than sue (Matthew 5:39). Accordingly, this book tells employers not to discriminate but does not exactly applaud employees who sue. I think the best way to prevent discrimination lawsuits is through effort by employers and employees. Most of the effort should come from employers. They should try harder to be race-blind, color-blind, gender-blind, age-blind, religion-blind, ethnicity-blind, and sexual orientation-blind when dealing with their employees. But some of the effort should come from employees. If some employees will try harder to be the best employee they can be, they will not be discriminated against. Effort by employers and employees will help employers prevent lawsuits and help employees prevent discrimination.

This book offers simple yet innovative mental exercises to help employers and employees develop a mentality that values diversity, legal compliance, the need for employees to earn a living, and the need for employers to earn a sufficient profit to justify staying in business.

Master and Servant?

Historically, the American legal system has referred to the employer-employee relationship as a "master-servant" relationship. "Master-servant" comes from the Bible. "Exhort servants to be obedient to their own masters, to be well pleasing in all things, not answering back, not pilfering, but showing all good fidelity," said Paul to Titus (Titus 2:9-10). "Masters, give your servants what is just and fair, knowing that you also have a Master in heaven," Paul told the Colossians (Colossians 4:1). "Servants, be submissive to your masters with all fear, not only to the good and gentle, but also to the harsh," Peter told the Pilgrims (1 Peter 2:18). I'm certainly not recommending that employers refer to employees as "servants." Employees would find it demeaning. Employers and employees should realize, however, that everyone who relies on others for a living is a "servant." That includes not only employees but also their bosses and company owners. It includes self-employed people. They all "serve" customers in one

10

way or another. In return, the customers pay them money. The money provides a living for these employees, bosses, and self-employed people. Most of the customers are "servants," too. That is how they acquire the money to begin with. From the wealthiest business owner down to the poorest laborer, everyone who works is a "servant" of someone else. There is nothing demeaning about that.

Chapter 2

Prevent Race Discrimination

"He has made from one blood every nation of men to
dwell on all the face of the earth."
Acts 17:26

"Racial superiority is a mere pigment of the
imagination."
Dr. Laurence J. Peter (author of The Peter Principle)

Almost Always Be Color-Blind

Employers should almost always be color-blind. Ignore
race and skin color completely, except in a few
situations I will discuss below. You should not even
mention race or skin color in the workplace unless you
really need to. If it is impossible for you to be color-
blind, be as color-blind as possible.

If you are a boss and you enjoy friendly,
constructive, well-intentioned discussions about race
and culture, try, if at all possible, to do it outside the
workplace and with people who are not your
employees. The book will have more to say about
diversity training, affirmative action, and
multiculturalism later in this chapter.

(This book uses the words "race" and "color"
interchangeably. Although the two words occasionally
have different meanings in the employment
discrimination context, they usually have the same

meaning. So when I say race, I also mean color, and when I say color, I also mean race. Most of what I say in this book about race and color also applies to ethnicity, national origin, and ancestry. There is considerable, though not total, overlap among those five words or terms.)

Some people don't want employers to be color-blind. They want employers to recognize, respect, and celebrate race and color. They believe that an employee's race, color, ethnicity, age, sex, religion, disability, and sexual orientation affect how the employee thinks, acts, and communicates. Some of them want you to communicate differently with black employees than you do with white employees. Some of them want reverse discrimination: They want you to hire a less-qualified job applicant of a certain race over a more-qualified job applicant of another race just to achieve racial diversity and to correct any past discrimination. Or they say color-blindness is impossible. "As long as people have eyes, they won't be color-blind," they say.

If they do not want employers to be, or at least try to be, color-blind, this presents a potential problem. The problem is racial profiling. Black people, particularly the Black Lives Matter movement, claim that police officers and employers do not treat black people as well as white people. Racial discrimination and racial profiling are, in my opinion, synonymous. In my opinion, the way to end racial profiling/discrimination is to train people to be color-blind. If people don't see color, they don't discriminate on the basis of color. As Carol Gilligan said in her famous book on male-female psychological differences, In a Different Voice: Psychological Theory and Women's Development: "[I]t is difficult to say 'different' without saying 'better' or 'worse.'" If you treat black people differently than white people, you increase the risk you will treat black people better, or worse, than white people. You increase the risk that a black person, or a white person, will sue you for race discrimination.

The law generally requires you to be color-blind when dealing with your employees. The primary federal employment discrimination law, Title VII of the Civil Rights Act of 1964, says:

> It shall be an unlawful employment practice for an employer to fail or refuse to hire or to discharge any individual, or otherwise to discriminate against any individual with respect to his compensation, terms, conditions, or privileges of employment, because of such individual's race, color, religion, sex, or national origin; or to limit, segregate, or classify his employees or applicants for employment in any way which would deprive or tend to deprive any individual of employment opportunities or otherwise adversely affect his status as an employee,

because of such individual's race, color, religion, sex, or national origin.

There are also federal laws pertaining to age discrimination, disability discrimination, and genetics discrimination. These laws will be discussed later in this book.

In my opinion—perhaps some people disagree with me on this—the law requires nondiscrimination more than it requires diversity. A diverse workforce is a very worthy goal. I value diversity very much. I will make recommendations in this book to help you achieve diversity. Our employment laws value diversity. But at the same time, our employment laws require nondiscrimination. Sometimes you must ask yourself: Do I want a diverse workforce, or do I want to prevent lawsuits? Sometimes you must choose between the two. The more you think about an employee's race or color, and especially if you make decisions based on an employee's race or color, the more you might achieve diversity but violate the law. I think legal compliance should be an employer's top priority. Achieving diversity should be a priority but not, in my opinion, as high a priority as legal compliance. I will, nonetheless, give you tips on how to achieve diversity.

There is another federal law that pertains exclusively to race discrimination and thus somewhat overlaps Title VII. This other federal law—the Civil Rights Act of 1866, as amended by the Civil Rights Act of 1991 (hereinafter CRA 1866)—pertains to the formation of contracts. The Supreme Court has held that for the purposes of CRA 1866, the employment relationship is a contract. Therefore, CRA 1866 applies to employers. CRA 1866 says, "All persons . . . shall have the same right . . . to make and enforce contracts . . . as is enjoyed by white citizens." That means that every citizen has the same employment rights that white citizens have. CRA 1866 applies to nearly all employers in the United States. That means that nearly all employers, even very small employers (or nearly all very small employers), in all states, are prohibited from discriminating against an employee on the basis of race or color. Being color-blind significantly reduces your risk of being sued for race discrimination.

The Bible commands us to be color-blind: "God created man in His own image...male and female" (Genesis 1:27). That means that all human beings, regardless of race or color, are created in God's image. It means all races and colors of humans are equally close to God. It means you should not treat one race better than another. "He has made from one blood every nation of men to dwell on all the face of the earth" (Acts 17:26).

On June 11, 1963, President John F. Kennedy addressed the nation to explain why he is sending National Guard troops to the University of Alabama. He wants the Guard to make sure that black students are allowed to enroll at the university. Later in his speech, Kennedy asked Congress "to make a commitment . . . to the proposition that race has no place in American life or law." Kennedy asked Congress to pass a civil rights act prohibiting race discrimination in employment, education, and public accommodations. He concluded his address by saying that black people "have the right to expect that the law will be fair, that the Constitution will be color blind." On August 28, 1963, Rev. Dr. Martin Luther King, Jr. addressed the nation. King said, "I have a dream that my four little children will one day live in a nation where they will not be judged by the color of their skin but by the content of their character." Unfortunately, Kennedy did not live to see the civil rights act become law. He was assassinated on November 22, 1963. Months later, the Civil Rights Act of 1964 became law. In 1968 Dr. King was assassinated.

The politics of "color-blindness" today (2018) are, in a way, the opposite of what they were in the 1960s. In the 1960s, liberals, blacks, and Democrats wanted a color-blind society. Kennedy (a Democrat) said so on June 11, 1963. King (a black man) said so on August 28, 1963. They called for legislation that would force society not to discriminate on the basis of race. Many (not all, but many) conservatives, whites, and Republicans opposed this legislation in 1963-64. In 2018, on the other hand, conservatives, whites, and Republicans tend to urge color-blindness while liberals, blacks, and Democrats urge celebration of, rather than blindness to, racial differences.

On July 21, 2016, Ivanka Trump said her father, Republican presidential nominee Donald Trump, is "color blind and gender neutral." On January 20, 2017,

President Trump said, "Whether we are black or brown or white, we all bleed the same red blood of patriots, we all enjoy the same glorious freedoms, and we all salute the same great American Flag. And whether a child is born in the urban sprawl of Detroit or the windswept plains of Nebraska, they look up at the same night sky, they fill their heart with the same dreams, and they are infused with the breath of life by the same almighty Creator." Affirmative action programs continue, rather than end, the focus on race and color. Whether and to what extent the federal government's affirmative action programs will continue during the Trump presidency remains to be seen.

The problem, or one problem, with focusing on race today (2018) is that the U.S. is not a "black and white" society anymore. It is harder to classify Americans by race today than it was in 1964. Racial integration has created many shades of skin color between black and white. In addition, America has many more Asians, Middle Easterners, and other people from around the world than America had in 1964. A person from India might have darker skin than an African American. In 1964, the person from India was in India. Today he is, or might be, in the United States. Does an American employer hire "blacks" when the employer hires people from India? What if the person from India marries an Irish-American and they conceive children? What race or color are their children? Some people call it "post-racial America." I don't use that term. To me, there is, and always has been, only one race: the human race.

In 2015 there was news of a white woman trying to look like a black woman. She was so convincing that she persuaded a chapter of the NAACP to make her its president. The important lesson from this episode: Don't make assumptions about people based on their race or color. Race and color tell you nothing about a particular individual.

The simplicity, if it ever was simple, of "black and white" is long gone. The more you think about race and skin color today, the more confused you will be. Obey the law. Be color-blind unless there is a very good, legally valid reason not to be color-blind. An example of a very good, legally valid reason not to be color-blind is if a government agency such as the U.S. Equal Employment Opportunity Commission (EEOC) requires you to provide the government with statistics about the racial composition of your workforce. The EEOC requires some employers to do so. To the extent that you need to notice, rather than be "blind" to, the race and skin color of your employees to comply with that requirement, do so. Do what the government requires. Another example, often related to the first example, is to comply with a government-mandated affirmative action plan.

Some people believe that you have a very good, legally valid reason not to be color-blind if your company discriminated against a racial group in the past. They argue that your company should now be race-conscious, not race-blind, and should now discriminate in favor of the group your company discriminated against in the past. I'll discuss this later in this chapter.

In general, though, you should, as much as legally possible, treat everyone as though they are the same race: the human race.

To those who argue that it is impossible to be color-blind (that is, they argue that it is impossible to ignore the race and skin color of your employees), I recommend that employers at least try to be color-blind. Even if you don't fully succeed in being color-blind, you should at least try to be color-blind. The more color-blind you are when dealing with your employees, the less discrimination there will be and the fewer employment discrimination lawsuits there will be. U.S. Supreme Court Chief Justice John Roberts said it well and simply in the case of Parents Involved in Community Schools v. Seattle School District No. 1 (2007): "The way to stop discrimination on the basis of race is to stop discriminating on the basis of race."

Some people think color-blindness means treating all people as though they are white. That is not what color-blindness means. Some people think color-blindness makes black people invisible. It does not. Color-blindness makes everyone equally visible. Color-blindness means being uninfluenced by whatever race or color a person happens to be. It means being uninfluenced by light ("white") skin, uninfluenced by dark ("black") skin, and uninfluenced by every shade of skin in between. It means regarding all people as belonging to one race: the human race. It means what

Barack Obama said at the 2004 Democratic National Convention: "There's not a black America and white America and Latino America and Asian America; there's the United States of America."

Some people argue that color-blindness is a form of racism because, they argue, color-blindness fails to take into account the history of racism in the United States and the importance to many people of their race and skin color. To those who argue that color-blindness is a form of racism, I respond: Then we are damned if we do and damned if we don't. If we take race into account when making personnel decisions, we violate the law. If we do not take race into account when making personnel decisions, we offend the people who believe that color-blindness is a form of racism.

You cannot please everybody. Your primary obligation is to comply with the law. In a democracy, the law reflects the will of the majority of the people. By being color-blind, you are pleasing the vast majority of Americans and complying with the law. Maybe you are not pleasing everybody, but it is impossible to please everybody. It is better to displease a few people than to violate the law and lose thousands of dollars in a discrimination lawsuit.

Furthermore, I am not urging total color-blindness. Blindness does not necessarily mean total lack of sight. A person can be legally blind yet still have some (limited) visual perception. This book acknowledges that there are a few possible exceptions to my suggestion to be color-blind. I'll discuss them later in this chapter.

How to Be Color-Blind

First, always keep in mind this fact: Skin color is just a sunscreen. Skin color has nothing to do with brainpower. Dark skin means that a person's distant ancestors were from a part of the world where it is sunny and hot most of the time, such as Africa or other places near the Earth's Equator. Dark skin was nature's way of protecting them from the sun's rays. Light skin means one's distant ancestors were from colder, less-sunny climates such as Scandinavia, Ireland, England, Poland, and Russia, and did not need such sun protection. Always keep in mind the following superb analysis that appeared in a 1997 New Haven Register article by Abram Katz entitled "One Race":

> Homo sapiens [human beings] originated in Eastern Africa about 200,000 years ago. Then, about 100,000 years ago, a group of this original population of modern humans left Africa and spread out among the world.
>
> [A]ll early modern humans probably appeared similar to populations in Africa, and then adapted to the different environments in which they settled.

"If you look at an ultraviolet map of the world, it correlates with human skin color," said [Nicholas] Bellantoni [then a University of Connecticut anthropology professor, now the State Archeologist of Connecticut].

Skin with sun-blocking dark pigment is a significant advantage to people in extremely sunny climates. However, people who settled in Northern Europe received less benefit from skin pigment, which they slowly lost.

For a more recent discussion, see Carl Zimmer, "A Single Migration from Africa Populated the World, Studies Find," New York Times, Sept. 21, 2016. Skin color is thus a function of climate, not brainpower. As the Catechism of the Catholic Church (paragraph 1934) states, "All men have the same nature and the same origin." As the Lutheran Church-Missouri Synod's statement "Racism and the Church" notes, "God created out of one man all members of the human family. . . . Racist lines of demarcation between human beings declaring some to be lesser members of humankind are, therefore, a blasphemous affront to our Creator."

Keep that in mind, and you will liberate yourself from prejudice.

The Bible does not say what race God is. To the extent that the Bible says anything at all about race, it regards the races as equal. This makes sense because

23

the number of white people and black people in the world is roughly equal. The number of Asians is even greater. We should all keep that in mind and treat the races equally.

Some people think God intended the races to be separate: whites in Europe, blacks in Africa, Asians in Asia. My understanding is that that may have been God's original intention—if you read Acts 17:26 in its entirety, not just the part I quoted above, you'll see what I mean—but He changed His mind after He was displeased with how things were going. His displeasure led Him to create the Great Flood. After the Great Flood, He told survivors of the Flood—the inhabitants of Noah's Ark—to "go out of the ark . . . and abound on the earth, and be fruitful and multiply on the earth" (Genesis 8:16-17). "Be fruitful and multiply, and fill the earth" (Genesis 9:1). So they did. They became whatever skin color best suited them to the climate.

Keep in mind that the Bible was written in the Middle East. The Middle East is where Europe, Africa, and Asia all meet. That is a sign that God is equally close to all three races. Each human being should regard the races as equal.

If anyone believes that God continues to want whites and blacks to live separately, that person should be reminded that blacks did not cause racial integration. Whites did. Whites captured (or "purchased") blacks in Africa in the 1700s and 1800s and brought them to America as slaves. Slavery ended in 1863. With slavery ended, whites should make sure that blacks have the same rights and opportunities whites have.

The same holds true regarding the Puerto Rican population. Like the black population, the Puerto Rican population did not all volunteer to become U.S. citizens. They were forced to become U.S. citizens. Many white Americans do not even know that Puerto Ricans are U.S. citizens. The United States wanted to control Puerto Rico so that no other nation (such as the former Soviet Union, which eventually gained a foothold in nearby Cuba) would. So the United States took control of Puerto Rico and made Puerto Ricans U.S. citizens. The United States should treat Puerto Ricans and white Americans as equal.

Some white Americans, especially those who emigrated—or whose parents or grandparents emigrated—to the United States from Europe or Asia complain when they hear Puerto Ricans speaking Spanish in Connecticut. They want Puerto Ricans to speak English in Connecticut. These white people ask, "Why don't they learn English? My parents came to the United States from (Russia, Italy, China, or wherever) and learned English. Why don't the Puerto Ricans learn English?" The answer is, first, most Puerto Ricans who live in Connecticut do speak English, but most of them also speak Spanish. Many prefer speaking Spanish. Second, unlike Europeans and Asians who came to the United States, Puerto Ricans did not really "come" to the United States. The United States made Puerto Rico a U.S. territory in order to further the strategic and military interests of the United States. A Puerto Rican has as much right to move to Connecticut as a Texan does, and the Puerto Rican should feel no more obligated to give up his Spanish language than the Texan does to give up his Texas (or Southern) accent. But at the same time, Puerto Ricans should realize that the more fluent they become in English, the more employment opportunities will be available to them in the 50 states. The most common language in most U.S. workplaces is English.

Here is another mental exercise. If you are a white manager and are contemplating firing a black employee, ask yourself: "If this black employee were white and performing the job exactly as he is performing it and saying the same things and exhibiting the same attitudes and behaviors as he is in fact saying and exhibiting, would I be firing this employee?" Think hard. If your answer is yes (that is, you would fire him), then you probably can fire him. If your answer is no, then don't fire him. If your answer is no, it means race is influencing your decision.

Here is another mental exercise. Don't "accentuate the negative." One element of racist thinking is to notice the race of a person only when the person does something bad or stupid but not notice it when the person does something good or smart. If a black person lets a white person cut in line in front of him in stalled traffic, the white person appreciates that, but the fact that this good person is black does not always register in the white person's mind. However, if the black person had not let the white person cut in, the white person would most likely have noticed that the "inconsiderate" person is black. If a white person is given the correct change by ten consecutive black store clerks but the wrong change by the eleventh one, the white person might fixate on the eleventh one. It probably did not occur to this white person that three of the last ten white store clerks also gave him the wrong change.

Here is another mental exercise. If you—a manager—hear or read a report that says blacks, on average, score lower on standardized tests in school (e.g., SATs) than whites and Asians do, don't be influenced by it when making managerial decisions. If you are at all influenced by it, allow it only to influence your thinking about the public school system, not employment. Occasionally we hear or read a report that says blacks, on average, score lower on SATs than whites and Asians do. Even if the report is accurate, it does not mean that blacks are less intelligent than whites and Asians. It does not mean that schools in black neighborhoods are inferior to schools in white neighborhoods. Maybe some schools are, but many schools are not. What it really means, I believe (my belief is supported by several articles in a book entitled "The Black-White Test Score Gap," published in 1998 by the Brookings Institution; and an article entitled "The Black-White Achievement Gap: When Progress Stopped," published in 2010 by Educational Testing Service) is that blacks (not all blacks, but many blacks) don't like taking these tests. Many blacks don't try their hardest on these tests. Why? Because they don't like being "tested" by whites, especially for no reason. Blacks enjoy school as much as whites and Asians do, and learn as much in school as whites and Asians do. But blacks are more likely to differentiate "testing" from schooling. They don't like being tested just for the sake of being tested. The purpose of the SAT is not to educate but to . . . test! Many blacks find it demeaning to be "tested" or "ranked" in school, especially when the tests and rankings are administered by whites. Being oppressed is bad enough. Being "tested" or "ranked" by the oppressor is even worse.

Employment tests are different. They are for the purpose of hiring. Blacks should have the same incentive to do well on employment tests as whites do. Consequently, it is okay for employers to hold black job applicants to the same standards as white job applicants when it comes to employment testing, so long as the tests are fair, job related, and not racially biased.

Hopefully these suggestions will help eliminate whatever tendency you might have to "accentuate the negative." Not everyone has this tendency, but some people do.

When Not to Be Color-Blind

For most employers, there are only two exceptions to the advice "Be colorblind." One is when you have two job applicants, one white and one black, who are equally qualified. If your company is overwhelmingly white, it may be wiser to hire the black applicant. Note that I said "may." It is possible there will be circumstances under which it will be wiser to hire the white applicant. But I think in most circumstances it will be wiser to hire the black applicant. In addition to the other benefits of diversity (it's good for business), diversity will help you if you or your company are ever sued for race discrimination by a black employee. An overwhelmingly white workforce—or an overwhelmingly white upper echelon within a company—will look suspicious to the EEOC, a judge, or a jury, particularly if you are located in an urban area with a sizeable black population. A diverse workforce tends to show that you do not discriminate against people of color.

But if the two applicants are not equally qualified, you should hire the better-qualified applicant—the applicant who, based on your objective appraisal of everything you know about him or her, you think would do the job better—whatever color that applicant happens to be. This definition of "better qualified" is, however, flexible. It gives you some leeway. If you have a predominantly white workforce and you have two job applicants, one white and one black, and it is a very close call which of them is better qualified, it may be wise to choose the black applicant. This is appropriate affirmative action.

What is inappropriate affirmative action—and illegal discrimination—is hiring a black person over a white person even though the white person is, by any objective standard, better qualified. There is an increasing number of reverse-discrimination cases: whites suing employers and educational institutions for hiring or admitting blacks who were less qualified than these white applicants. Many whites are winning these cases.

The second exception comes into play if you have terminated a black employee. It may be wise to hire a black person to replace him or her. It is difficult (not impossible, but difficult) for a terminated black employee to claim that the employer is prejudiced against blacks if the employer replaced that employee with a black person.

A third possible exception—although I urge you to exercise great caution with this one—is to correct any past discrimination that has occurred in your workplace. If your company discriminated against blacks in the past, one can argue that it is a good idea for your company to discriminate in favor of blacks now. There is an EEOC regulation, 29 C.F.R. (Code of Federal Regulations) section 1608.3(b), that seems to encourage this. But in my opinion, the regulation does not make clear exactly how and when a company should do this. Does discriminating in favor of blacks mean discriminating against whites? Title VII makes it illegal to discriminate against anyone (white, black, or other) on the basis of race. The employer who wants to rectify past discrimination by engaging in current or future discrimination must first adopt a written affirmative action (AA) plan, according to 29 C.F.R.

section 1608.4(d)(1). But some obvious questions arise. Should you declare in the AA plan that your company discriminated against blacks in the past? I urge you to be very cautious about this. Discuss it with your lawyer.

Another exception is if an employer is operating under a consent decree or government contract that requires the employer to hire more people of color.

Another exception, of sorts, applies if the government asks you to count and report how many women and people of color you employ. Some employers are required to do this, including most employers with 100 or more employees and most employers with substantial government contracts. You can then ask each employee what his or her race is, and if he or she declines to answer, you can visually guess what race he or she is. This is not really "considering" race or sex. It is just counting and reporting.

The mere fact that an employer has chosen, or is required, to be an "affirmative action" employer does not mean that the employer must hire less-qualified people of color over better-qualified white employees. "Affirmative action" is a highly misunderstood term. Some think it means "reverse discrimination": hiring a less-qualified job applicant over a more-qualified applicant just because the less-qualified applicant belongs to an historically oppressed or underrepresented group, such as an ethnic minority or the female sex. Many whites and males are opposed to reverse discrimination.

But the true meaning of affirmative action is simply taking extra steps to ensure that women and minority-group members know about your job openings and feel welcome to apply for and perform jobs in your workplace. Affirmative action of this latter type is perfectly legal, proper, and advisable. Keep in mind that the workforce is not becoming whiter, younger, or more male. It is becoming more female, racially diverse, and older. Diversity is good. The more your workplace reflects these new demographics, the harder it will be for people to accuse you of racism.

Another advantage of diversity is that you can probably attract more customers if you hire a diverse workforce. You might, for example, attract more black customers if you hire more black employees. You might attract more female and Asian customers if you hire more women and Asians. But if you base hiring and promotion decisions on customers' racial preference, or on what you perceive to be customers' racial preference, you might run into legal trouble.

Consider what happened to national drug-store chain Walgreens in 2007. Walgreens has stores in many poor, inner-city neighborhoods. Walgreens is perhaps the last company you would expect to be sued for race discrimination. But that is exactly what happened. Walgreens was sued by some of its black managers (and by the U.S. Equal Employment Opportunity Commission) for race discrimination in 2007 because, the suit alleged, Walgreens tried to make sure that its stores in black neighborhoods had black managers.

Walgreens was doing what many diversity trainers encourage employers to do. But some black managers sued, alleging that the stores in black neighborhoods generated less revenue, and therefore lower pay for managers, than some stores in white neighborhoods, and they argued that Walgreens should have assigned them to these higher-revenue stores in white neighborhoods. In 2008, Walgreens settled the suit by agreeing to pay $24 million to a group of some 10,000 black Walgreens employees and former employees.

The lesson to be learned from the Walgreens case: The best way to avoid being accused of race discrimination is to be color-blind when making employment decisions. The more you notice, think about, and make managerial decisions based on the race or color of your employees, the more legal trouble you potentially bring upon yourself.

For employees who work for the federal government, President Obama's diversity initiative (Executive Order 13583, entitled "Government-Wide Diversity and Inclusion Strategic Plan 2011") says the government should try to achieve diversity—that is, try to build a work force from all segments of society— "while avoiding discrimination for or against any employee or applicant on the basis of race, color, religion, sex (including pregnancy or gender identity), national origin, age, disability, sexual orientation or any other prohibited basis." The best way for private-sector employers to prevent employment discrimination lawsuits is to do the same: Try to achieve diversity while avoiding discrimination for or against an employee or applicant on a prohibited basis. Logic dictates that the best way to do that is to be color-blind; you should be color-blind unless there is a very good, legally valid reason not to be color-blind.

Diversity Training?

This book neither encourages nor discourages "diversity training." There are many types of diversity training. Some are helpful. Others are counterproductive. If you bring in a diversity trainer, do not express negative, prejudicial, or stereotypical feelings about any group—even if you have such feelings—during training or at any other time. The less you say about race in the workplace, the better. Let the diversity trainer do most if not all the talking. Any such talk on your part can be used against you in court to prove that you are racist or prejudiced. Diversity training is more desirable if done for the purpose of preparing employees to do business in foreign countries.

Be careful if you use the words "culture" and "multiculturalism." People who use those words are usually talking about race and color but think "culture" and "multiculturalism" are more "politically correct" than "race" and "color." Increasingly, the word "culture" is being used to sugar-coat old stereotypes and overgeneralizations. It nearly always means something other than culture. If not race or color, then language, national origin, sex, geography, religion, economic class, sexual orientation, or something else.

"Culture" and "multiculturalism" are used to justify comments like, "Germans are very punctual but Italians tend to be late; it's their culture." "That is part of the male culture." "People in New York eat dinner late; that is their culture." "Asians do not like to make eye contact; it is against their culture." Korean culture is this or that. Puerto Ricans like this or that. Irish, Jews, Southerners, Northerners, whatever.

Ignore such generalizations. People are people. Some Germans are punctual and some are late. Some New Yorkers eat dinner late, others eat early. People think and communicate differently from one another in the workplace, but it rarely has anything to do with their race, color, ethnicity, sex, age, religion, genetics, disability, or sexual orientation. Someone can be your exact age, ethnicity, profession, sex, religion, economic background, and live on your street, but you will not necessarily like him or her or agree with him or her on anything. Conversely, someone different from you racially, religiously, professionally, economically, sexually, and in every other "cultural" way might be a close friend of yours and agree with you on most things.

I taught at the University of New Haven (Connecticut) for nine years, 2005-2014. I had a total of approximately 2,000 students. They were as diverse as any 2,000 college students in the U.S. could possibly be. When I looked at a large classroom of students, I felt I was looking at the world. Their racial and ethnic composition was as close to the racial and ethnic composition of the world as any 40 (or whatever number were in my class at the time) people enrolled in an American university can possibly be. Of the 40, approximately 20 were international students. Many were white, many were black, many were Asian, and many were a combination. In my opinion, there was no difference whatsoever in the way they thought, wrote, and spoke, with the slight exception that some of the international students spoke and wrote English in a way that hinted they were not born and raised in the U.S. Were all my students alike? No. They differed from each other the way any person differs from another person. But those differences, in my opinion, had nothing whatsoever to do with race, ethnicity, or skin color. Had I been blindfolded, so I had no idea what any student looked like, and I heard every comment that every student made in class, and I read, outside of class with the blindfold off, all their exams and papers, I would not know who is white, who is black, who is a color in between, who is American, who is Central or South American, who is African, who is European, and who is Asian. For that matter, I also would not know who is Christian, who is Jewish, who is Muslim, who is gay, who is heterosexual, etc. The only way I would know who is male and who is female is by listening to their voices, and even then I often would not know. Listening to the students, I would in some instances know who is an international student, because of their foreign accent, but I doubt I could tell you what country they are from. Reading their papers, I could not begin to guess any of these categories. I would not use the word "culture" to describe anything about the students.

In the workplace, the less you think about and talk about race, color, ethnicity, sex, age, religion, genetics, disability, and sexual orientation, the better. Keep in mind the words of Marcel Marceau, who as a pantomime artist performed silently onstage but spoke normally offstage. He said, "There is no French way of laughing and no American way of crying."

Exercise some caution if you reject job applicants based on their criminal record. In Connecticut, "No employer shall inquire about a prospective employee's prior arrests, criminal charges or convictions on an initial employment application, unless (1) the employer is required to do so by an applicable state or federal law, or (2) a security or fidelity bond or an equivalent bond is required for the position for which the prospective employee is seeking employment." Conn. General Statutes § 31-51i(b). After the initial employment application, the employer can inquire but should be cautious. The EEOC, in an enforcement guidance dated April 25, 2012 ("Consideration of Arrest and Conviction Records in Employment Decisions Under Title VII of the Civil Rights Act of 1964"), has taken the position that some such rejections are racially discriminatory. The laws pertaining to applicants for jobs with the State of Connecticut might be somewhat different than the laws pertaining to private-sector employers in this regard.

Don't Talk About Race and Skin Color Except When Necessary

When people, even people who are strong supporters of civil rights and racial equality, comment about a race or ethnicity other than their own, their comment is likely to lead to hard feelings and negative consequences unless the comment is 100 percent positive.

The Target store chain—or, at least, one warehouse in the chain—was embarrassed in 2013 when three former employees who sued Target for race/ethnicity discrimination revealed a document entitled "Employee and Labor Relations Multi-Cultural Tips," which they (the three employees) claim Target distributed to managers. The document seemed to be well-intentioned. It seemed to be designed to reduce or eliminate prejudice against Hispanic employees. It pointed out that not all Hispanics eat tacos and burritos, not all Hispanics dance to salsa, and so on. But this document was used against Target in this lawsuit. It was used in an effort to show that Target discriminates against Hispanics. This is another example of why you should not talk about race and color except when necessary. Even well-intentioned discussions about race and color can lead to legal trouble. Perhaps some good might result from this type of diversity training, but it seems to me that it is outweighed by the potential harm to the company. The bottom line: Be very careful if you do diversity training.

Can racial and ethnic diversity be achieved without talking about race and ethnicity? I will answer that question this way: Employers should make a strong effort to achieve racial diversity except when such effort leads to race discrimination (race discrimination being defined as treating an employee—white, black, or other—less favorably due to his or her race or ethnicity). The more that race, ethnicity, sex, age, religion, genetics, disability, and sexual orientation are discussed in the workplace, the more lawsuits there are.

Over the past 50 years or so, there have been countless conversations, dialogues, workshops, and other well-intentioned discussions about race, but it is unclear whether they have reduced race discrimination in the workplace. The best way to end or reduce race discrimination in the workplace is to be color-blind. Efforts to be color-blind will not always succeed, but conversations, dialogues, and workshops on race never, or hardly ever, succeed. In the workplace, being color-blind, or at least trying to be color-blind, is more apt to succeed than talking about race is.

Summary

This discussion ("Almost always be color-blind") boils down to the following simple advice. When firing, laying off, demoting, or disciplining employees, or when setting pay or other terms and conditions of employment, be totally color-blind. In other words, when taking negative or neutral action, be color-blind.

When recruiting, hiring, or promoting employees, be color-blind except when the qualifications of a black candidate and a white candidate are equal or very close (too close to call), in which case you probably (there might be an occasional exception to this; talk to your lawyer about particular situations) should opt for diversity: If you have a shortage of black employees at that particular job level, you should probably hire the black candidate. In other words, when taking positive action, you ordinarily (again, there might be an occasional exception to this; talk to your lawyer about particular situations) can, when the qualifications of two job applicants are equal or very close (too close to call), give some consideration to color and become more diverse. But even so, try not to talk about race or color.

Do not talk about race except when necessary.

Chapter 3

Prevent Sex Discrimination

> "She considers a field and buys it; from her
> profits she plants a vineyard. She girds
> herself with strength, and strengthens her
> arms. She perceives that her merchandise is
> good."
>
> Proverbs 31:16-18

Treat Men and Women the Same (With a Few Very Minor Exceptions)

The topic of sex discrimination has become a bit confusing over the past few years. That is because not everyone defines the words "men," "women," "male," "female," "his," "her," "sex," and "gender" today the way they did a few years ago. To some people today, a male is a person who feels like or identifies as a male, regardless of the person's sex at birth. I'll discuss this more in Chapter 8 (Prevent Sexual Orientation Discrimination). In this book, when I say "sex," I mean sex at birth: male or female. When I say "man," "male," or "he," I mean the traditional, anatomical definition of those words. I mean a person with a penis. When I say "woman," "female," or "she," I mean a person with a vagina. I read Genesis 1:27 to mean that every person is created male or female and stays that way. I realize that not everyone agrees with me about that.

Some people opine that "sex" and "gender" are two different things. I see no reason to get into that discussion here. I occasionally use the words interchangeably. For example, I discuss "gender-neutral" language in this chapter.

I have read (not in the Bible) that an infinitesimally small number of people are "intersex," meaning their sex at birth is not clearly male or female. I do not know enough about them to comment on them, except to say this: The law applies to and protects every person, including intersex persons.

Try not to differentiate in any way between men and women in the workplace. Whether you differentiate between men and women in the bedroom, restroom, golf course, or other places is another topic; I will not comment on it in this book. In the workplace—where people actually work (I don't mean the restroom)—try not to differentiate between men and women. You can use different pronouns (he, she) and salutations (Mr., Ms., etc.) for men and women. You can provide separate restrooms for men and women. You can allow, and sometimes require, men and women to dress differently. (I'll discuss the transgender issue in chapter 8.) But otherwise you should pretend that all your workers are the same sex. The law says you should treat women and men the same in the workplace. If the woman is pregnant and close to giving birth or has just given birth, she may have some rights that men don't have (see Pregnancy, Adoption, and Maternity Leave below). If there is a job that can only be performed by one sex, you can hire that sex, and you need not hire the other sex, for that job. For example, if you need someone to model women's clothes, you can restrict your hiring to women for that position. That is called a "bona fide occupational qualification," or "BFOQ." Use gender-neutral language as much as reasonably possible in oral and written communication. Don't call women over the age of 18 "girls."

If you are a man contemplating firing a woman, ask yourself: "If this employee were a man rather than a woman, would I be firing this employee?" If your answer is yes (that is, you would fire this employee), you probably can fire her. If your answer is no, don't fire her. If your answer is no, it means sex/gender is influencing your decision. With very, very few exceptions, there is no reason to treat women differently than men.

This advice to treat men and women the same might upset some people. After years of trying—successfully—to prove that men and women have equal abilities, some people (some women and some men) are now saying that women think, communicate, and manage employees differently than men do. Employers should ignore such talk. For thousands of years, one major cause of discrimination against women was the belief that women think differently than men. That belief resulted in women earning less than men and being subordinate to men in many types of employment. In the 1970s and '80s, women rejected that belief. As a result, women made great strides toward achieving full equality with men in the workplace. Today, however, that belief is back in vogue in some circles.

Keep in mind that that belief—the belief that women think, communicate, and manage employees differently than men do—is held and expressed mainly by authors, lecturers, and college professors, not managers. Managers should not hold or express that belief. Managers who express that belief or base their managerial decisions on that belief risk being sued for sex discrimination. If you are a manager, you should ignore all statements and literature that argue that women think, communicate, or manage differently than men do. Such arguments are generalizations that ignore the fact that not all men are the same and not all women are the same. Moreover, these generalizations are usually based on immeasurable characteristics and anecdotal observations.

These generalizations are nothing new. They are as old as time. They have historically hurt women more than helped women in the quest for equality. Examples of such generalizations are: "Women use their instincts and emotional intelligence more than men do. Men just use logic." "Women prefer working in groups; men prefer working alone." "Women are less assertive than men." "Women are more nurturing than men." "Women are better communicators than men." "Men are better negotiators than women." "Men don't ask directions." "Men don't cry." "Men's brains are 'hard-wired,' which makes them less comfortable expressing their emotions." "Men can only think about one thing at a time; women can think about many things at a time." "Women think 'outside the box' better than men do."

The people who make such statements mean well. They are trying to empower women. But in fact they are doing the opposite: They are perpetuating old stereotypes about women, such as the stereotype that men use logic more than instinct while women use instinct more than logic. Remember the old stereotype of a woman complaining to her husband, "I hate it when you're logical"? These people are claiming that that is true: men are too logical. "Men should use less logic and more feelings and intuition, like women do," these people say. Such statements lead to legal trouble. If a male manager were to say "Men think logically more than women do," he would be accused of "degrading" and "devaluing" women. He might get sued for sex discrimination. He would face an uphill battle in court.

You should treat men and women the same and not talk about sex differences at all. In fact, you should assume (except perhaps in some very rare circumstances) that in terms of job performance, there are no sex differences.

Women managers who talk about how women are better at one thing or another than men are (such as having better "intuition," "listening skills," or "communication skills" than men) risk being sued for sex discrimination by male subordinates and rejected male job applicants. They might even be sued for creating a "hostile work environment" toward men. Women should avoid such talk. Such talk will cause men to file sex discrimination lawsuits.

Men and Women Are Both from Earth

Managers should reject all generalizations that men are this and women are that. Such generalizations are no different than generalizations claiming that white people are this and black people are that. Such generalizations only lead to trouble. Such generalizations come dangerously close to saying, "Women are better than men" or "Men are smarter than women." That is no different from saying, "Blacks are better than whites" or "Whites are smarter than blacks" or some other rash, racist, sexist generalization. It is dangerous stuff. As Carol Gilligan warned in her famous book on male-female psychological differences, "In a Different Voice: Psychological Theory and Women's Development," "[I]t is difficult to say 'different' without saying 'better' or 'worse.'"

Don't accept unquestioningly the "studies" showing gender differences. There are all kinds of "studies" showing that women are different than men, blacks are different than whites, old people are different than young people, etc. A hundred years ago, policymakers sometimes used such studies to justify discrimination against blacks, women, Jews, and other "minorities." Hitler allegedly cited "studies" to justify his racist thoughts and actions. Today, such studies are more often used for benevolent purposes, but they are often confusing. "In One Ear, Without the Other" was an article that appeared some years ago. It was about an Indiana University School of Medicine study that showed that men listen with the left side of their brains while women listen with both sides of their brains. The first line of the article read, "Score one for exasperated women: New research suggests men really do listen with just half their brains." Numerous women, and some men, went on talk shows and declared that this study proves once and for all that men "just don't listen." But men countered by saying that in reality the study shows that men have more brainpower than women: Men need only half their brains to hear as much as women hear with their whole brains. Managers should ignore such studies and debates.

Here is another example. An article in the December 2007 Harvard Business Review discussed a study that concluded that women are more apt to accept the first salary offer from an employer than to negotiate with the employer for a higher salary. The article said, "[W]omen and men negotiate differently for pay raises, promotions, and salaries. The key difference: Many women don't negotiate at all." A manager—male or female—might read that article and decide not to put women on any negotiating team. According to the study, or to the article about the study, women are too willing to accept what is offered rather than negotiate for more. A manager (male or female) might read that article and decide to offer lower salaries to women than to men, believing, as the article asserts, that women are more likely to accept a lower salary than men are. Such managerial thinking is discriminatory and can lead to discrimination lawsuits.

With all due respect to the people who conduct and write about such studies and debates, employers should disregard such studies and debates. Such studies and debates lead to feuds and discrimination. They create friction rather than unity. There is often a fine line between statistics and stereotypes. There are studies and statistics showing that certain ethnic groups have more athletic ability, mathematical ability, and some other abilities and traits than other ethnic groups do. "Study finds ethnic link to math test scores," was a headline a few years ago. "How race affects smoking," which cites a study showing that certain ethnic groups have more difficulty quitting smoking than other ethnic groups do, is another. The September 2013 Harvard Business Review had an article entitled, "How Women Decide." Whether there is or is not a link between ethnicity and math scores, or between race and quitting smoking, or between gender and decisionmaking, and whether that link, if it exists, is due to one factor or another factor, employers should ignore it. Employers who rely on such studies and let these studies guide their behavior at work are asking for trouble—legal trouble. Big legal trouble. Employers should disregard all studies, books, seminars, and discussions that show intellectual or emotional differences between men and women, whites and blacks, old people and young people, etc.

Employers should disregard statements to the effect that men were "brought up" one way and women the other way. Some men were, some weren't. Some women were, some weren't. Furthermore, not every man and woman does what they were "brought up" to do.

In short, employers should disregard all generalizations about men and all generalizations about women. Generalizing is stereotyping, and stereotyping leads to discrimination. The more you discriminate or differentiate between men and women or between one race and another race, the more legal trouble you potentially bring upon yourself. You should not differentiate between men and women except you can differentiate in the four aspects listed above—dress codes, restrooms, maternity leave, and bona fide occupational qualification ("BFOQ")—or between whites and people of color. To "differentiate" is basically to discriminate, and discrimination is usually against a group, or in favor of one group at the expense of another group. Regarding dress codes, in some states, including Connecticut, a man might have the legal right to dress like a woman, and a female employee might have the legal right to dress like a man, at work. I'll discuss this in the chapter Prevent Sexual Orientation Discrimination. Few employers object to a woman wearing pants, but many employers object to a man wearing a skirt or dress, especially at work.

The "BFOQ" exception to the rule that men and women must be treated the same is a very narrow exception. Only if all members of a sex (all men or all women) are disqualified for a job can you restrict your hiring to the other sex. It happens very rarely.

If college professors wish to conduct experiments to see if men think differently than women, that is okay. If teachers and trainers want to help people learn to value or even just tolerate diversity, that too is okay. Everyone should value or at least tolerate diversity. In your behavior, however—at least in the workplace—you should treat men and women the same.

For all these reasons, this book recommends against diversity training that deals with sex or gender (or religion or sexual orientation, for that matter). Perhaps if you have some employees who do business in certain foreign countries where, by law, women are treated differently than men, those employees might benefit from such training as it relates to those specific countries.

Some men (and some women) believe that equality for women in the workplace conflicts with the Bible. They are mistaken. They base their belief on biblical passages that they believe give husbands more authority than wives in the home. But regardless of whether their interpretation of those passages is correct, those passages do not give men more authority than women in the workplace. Even the Southern Baptist Convention, which issued a policy statement in 2000 declaring that wives should "graciously submit" to their husbands, does not advocate or tolerate sex discrimination in the workplace.

God designed us so that only women get pregnant and nurse babies, which leads some men (and some women) to believe that women were designed to stay home with children while men go out to work. But remember, God also gave men and women the same brainpower, brainpower that has created a modern world that values thinking more than brawn. Thus it is perfectly natural for women in modern times to work outside the home just as men do. Of course, as the proverb at the top of this chapter indicates, it was perfectly natural in biblical times as well.

Indeed, Catholic schools and hospitals have been run by women for centuries (including direct supervision over doctors). The United Methodist Church has declared, "We affirm women and men to be equal in every aspect of their common life. We therefore urge that every effort be made to eliminate sex-role stereotypes in activity and portrayal of family life. We affirm the right of women to equal treatment in employment, responsibility, promotion, and compensation." The Presbyterian Church U.S.A. advocates "full inclusiveness and equality [between men and women] in the church and in society."

As for brawn, few jobs require such enormous physical strength that women cannot perform them as well as men. If you need to fill a job that requires enormous physical strength, do not assume, just because an applicant is female, that she is weaker than the male applicants. You can, if you want, conduct strength and endurance tests if such tests are job-related. Everyone, male and female, will take the tests. The strongest applicants will get the jobs, be they male or female. Of course, you are not required to conduct such tests. But if a 150-pound man and a 150-pound woman apply for a job, don't assume that the man is stronger. Let them both test for the job. The test does not have to be elaborate or lengthy. It can be short and simple. Don't have a height, weight, or strength requirement unless you have substantial proof that a certain height, weight, or strength is necessary to perform the job. Some police and fire departments might still have height or weight requirements, but that is government (public-sector) employment. Sometimes the rules are a bit different in public-sector employment than in private-sector employment.

If a test procedure screens out a protected group (for example, if all or almost all women, or all or almost all blacks, flunk the test, and all or almost all men, or all or almost all whites, pass the test), you should explore whether there is an equally effective alternative selection procedure that has less adverse impact on women or blacks, and if so, adopt the alternative procedure. You should explore whether another test would predict job performance but not disproportionately exclude women or blacks. To ensure that a test or selection procedure remains predictive of success in a job, you should keep abreast of changes in job requirements and update the test specifications and selection procedures accordingly. You should ensure that tests and selection procedures are not adopted casually by managers who know little about these processes. A test or selection procedure can be an effective management tool, but no test or selection procedure should be implemented without an understanding of its effectiveness and limitations for the organization, its appropriateness for a specific job, and whether it can be appropriately administered and scored.

The law generally (there might be an occasional exception to this) allows you to discriminate on the basis of physical attractiveness. You can hire a pretty woman over a not-so-pretty woman if you want, and you can hire a handsome man over a not-so-handsome man if you want. However, if you do, make sure that you do not consciously or subconsciously discriminate on the basis of sex, race, ethnicity, age, religion, disability, or sexual orientation. If you are more apt to judge women as good looking than you are men, and thus are more apt to hire women than men for a particular type of job, that is sex discrimination and is illegal. If you are more apt to judge white people as good looking than you are black people, or more apt to judge young people as good looking than you are old people, that is race discrimination or age discrimination and is illegal. Keep up with developments in the law on this topic. There are efforts being made in some states to enact legislation that would altogether prohibit discrimination based on physical appearance. Thus, it is possible that sometime soon employers in one or more states will be prohibited from discriminating on the basis of an employee's physical attractiveness.

No law requires that your workforce reflect the sex ratio (roughly 50% male, 50% female) of the general population. As a matter of common sense, however, an all-male or nearly all-male workforce does raise the suspicion that you discriminate against women. If you have such a workforce and a male and a female with roughly equal qualifications apply for a job, it may be wiser to hire the female. The more women you employ, especially in high places, the harder it is to accuse you of discriminating against women.

And be on the lookout for men claiming they are being discriminated against by women in overwhelmingly female workplaces. If a man with good secretarial skills applies for a secretarial job at your company and all ten of your secretaries are female, and you reject the man for the job, don't be surprised if he sues for sex discrimination. He might even win.

Pregnancy, Adoption, and Maternity Leave

The law generally regards pregnancy discrimination as a form of sex discrimination. You should treat pregnant employees at least as well, and sometimes better, than you treat employees with a short-term illness. Connecticut law requires employers to allow pregnant women time off to give birth and recuperate ("maternity leave") even if they would not ordinarily allow a male employee or a not-pregnant female employee that much time off for illness. Unless the law or an employer's particular arrangement with his or her employees

54

provides otherwise, the employer does not have to pay the woman during this period. If the employer has 50 or more employees, an employee who is the parent (male or female) of a newborn (or newly adopted) or soon-to-be-born child might be entitled to up to 16 weeks off, under the federal and Connecticut family and medical leave acts (FMLA). Pregnancy-related illnesses (such as morning sickness) ordinarily do not qualify as "disabilities" under the federal Americans with Disabilities Act, so the ADA provides little protection to pregnant women. But Connecticut and some other states require employers to reasonably accommodate pregnant employees the way they accommodate disabled employees.

The Connecticut Department of Labor has written a new poster that Connecticut employers are required to post beginning in January 2018. It says each employer with more than 3 employees must comply with the anti-discrimination and reasonable accommodation laws related to an employee or job applicant's pregnancy, childbirth, or related conditions, including lactation. The employer cannot discriminate against an employee or job applicant because of her pregnancy, childbirth or other related conditions (e.g., breastfeeding or expressing milk at work). Prohibited discriminatory conduct includes:

- Terminating employment because of pregnancy, childbirth or related condition

- Denying reasonable leave of absence for disability due to pregnancy (e.g., doctor prescribed bed rest during 6-8 week recovery period after birth); there is no requirement that the employee be employed for a certain length of time prior to being granted job protected leave of absence under this law.

- Denying disability or leave benefits accrued under plans maintained by the employer

- Failing to reinstate employee to original job or equivalent position after leave

- Limiting, segregating or classifying the employee in a way that would deprive her of employment opportunities

- Discriminating against her in the terms or conditions of employment.

Connecticut employers (with 3 or more employees) must provide a reasonable accommodation to an employee or job applicant due to her pregnancy, childbirth or needing to breastfeed or express milk at work. Reasonable accommodations include, but are not limited to:

- Being permitted to sit while working

- More frequent or longer breaks

- Periodic rest

- Assistance with manual labor

- Job restructuring

- Light duty assignments

- Modified work schedules

- Temporary transfers to less strenuous or less hazardous work

- Time off to recover from childbirth (prescribed by a doctor, typically 6-8 weeks

- Break time and appropriate facilities (not a bathroom) for expressing milk.

No Connecticut employer may discriminate against employee or job applicant by denying a reasonable accommodation due to pregnancy. Prohibited discriminatory conduct includes:

- Failing to make reasonable accommodation, unless such accommodation is an undue hardship. To demonstrate an undue hardship, the employer must show that the accommodation would require a significant difficulty or expense in light of its circumstances.

- Denying job opportunities to employee or job applicant because of request for reasonable accommodation

- Forcing employee or job applicant to accept a reasonable accommodation when she has no known limitation related to pregnancy or the accommodation is not required to perform the essential duties of job

- Requiring employee to take a leave of absence where a reasonable accommodation could have been made instead.

Connecticut employers are prohibited from retaliating against an employee because of a request for reasonable accommodation.

Some pregnancy-related illnesses may qualify as "serious health conditions" entitling a pregnant woman (and possibly her spouse) to FMLA leave, but

58

others will not. If employers allow men who are injured on the job to work light duty jobs, the employer must allow pregnant women to work light duty jobs if necessary.

Employers should not discriminate against pregnant women or women who might become pregnant. Not only is it illegal, it is counterproductive. Although pregnancy might occasionally divert a woman's time and attention away from her work, and giving birth will keep her out of the workplace for a few months, pregnancy and childbirth also give her an added incentive to do a good job for you. She now has another mouth to feed. She will need more money than a childless person does. She will be motivated to work harder to earn that extra money. She might seek a promotion or pay raise. The same is true of men whose wives get pregnant. These men have more incentive, too.

Thus, discrimination against women due to their pregnancy or potential pregnancy is bad not only from a legal standpoint but also from a business standpoint. Many working mothers have very good child-care arrangements. According to Journal of the American Board of Family Medicine, 58 percent of employed, first-time mothers giving birth in the United States between 2001 and 2003 returned to work within three months after giving birth, and according to a 1999 edition of Working Mother magazine (I don't know if the percentage has changed since 1999), 83 percent of employed, first-time mothers returned to work within six months after giving birth. Many companies are allowing women (and men) to bring their babies to work and are providing onsite child care facilities. Many women want to earn as much money as their husbands earn. Equal earnings mean equal power in the marital relationship. More and more men are content with having less power than their wives have. If their wives have successful careers, these men are willing to spend more time at home with the children. If the woman has a high-paying job, she and her husband might decide that her career will come first. Many male executives say, "I wish my wife had a high-paying job; then I could stay home more. I'd rather be home with my kids than working so hard." As Jane Bryant Quinn said in a column about married couples, "When she brings home more bacon, he makes more beds."

What can pregnant women do to reduce the likelihood they will be discriminated against? Here is some good advice given to pregnant job seekers by Elaine Varelas, a career counselor in Boston, in the "Job Doc" section of the May 31, 2009, Boston Globe:

> Mother Nature lets you keep the news private for some time, and during those months I would network and interview without disclosing your situation. Some employers might not agree with this advice. I can tell you that the disclosure of this news—legal or not—does affect how people view you as a candidate. As a good job seeker, you need to spend time with a

potential employer so they can see what you have to offer and how you would fit into their culture before they are faced with any obstacles—which a maternity represents to some employers.

As you move into second and third interviews, and the second and third trimesters, you are right to feel the need to begin disclosing your situation, and a very strong statement about your plans to return to work. If this is not your first child, hiring managers need to know that you returned to work after your previous leaves. Potential employers need to hear about the plans you have for child care and backup care. They need to hear that you have sisters or close friends who have also gone back to work after having children and that you learned a great deal about how you will handle the situation from them.

Some employers will assume you have no idea how you will feel leaving your newborn, and they will be very hesitant about investing training dollars in what they view as a high-risk hire. Depending on how far along you are, you may be able to negotiate a project or temporary arrangement with them prior to having your child, with a formal start date following your leave.

> I have seen some great hires of talented women while they were pregnant. The managers and organizations who took this "risk" were able to get exceptional employees with unbelievable loyalty.

I think that is generally good advice, although it is difficult to generalize about what employers think and what job seekers should do. It will depend on your particular circumstances.

One More Tip for Employers

If you fire a woman, it may be wise to hire a woman to replace her, especially if you have a mostly male workforce. It will be much harder for the fired woman to claim sex discrimination. You are not required to replace her with a woman, but it may be wise to do so, especially if you have few women employees in that job category.

Chapter 4

Prevent Sexual Harassment

"Do not use liberty as an opportunity for the flesh."
Galatians 5:13

The above passage from Galatians means, in employer-employee relations: Don't use your power (liberty) as an employer to gain sexual access to your employee.

Sexual harassment was one of the biggest stories of 2017. Thousands of women came forward with complaints about men sexually harassing them. Dozens of famous, powerful men were fired or pressured to resign their jobs as a result.

There are two types of sexual harassment, but it is not always easy to distinguish one from the other. Nor is there much reason to. You can be sued for either. The two types are 1) quid pro quo sexual harassment and 2) sexually hostile work environment.

Quid Pro Quo Sexual Harassment

"Quid pro quo" sexual harassment occurs when a boss makes employment decisions based on whether a subordinate will have sexual (or romantic) relations with him. It need not be as explicit as "Go to bed with me or you're fired." If a boss asks a secretary for a date and she turns him down, and a year later he fires her for being late for the fifteenth time (after giving her stern warnings the twelfth, thirteenth, and fourteenth times), don't be surprised if she sues him and the company for quid pro quo sexual harassment. She will claim that the real reason he fired her is that she refused to go out with him a year earlier. If she does date him for awhile, and the relationship then turns sour, and he fires her for being late the fifteenth time, she will claim that the real reason he fired her is that the relationship turned sour.

For that reason, supervisors generally should not date, or have sex with, their subordinates, or even try to. If you are physically attracted to your secretary or other subordinate, try to get him or her off your mind in that respect. Try to avoid thinking of him or her in a sexual way. There is too great a chance that such a romantic relationship, even if occurs for awhile, will eventually end. When it ends, you will never be able to discipline or fire that subordinate without being accused of sexual harassment or "retaliation." It is illegal to fire an employee in retaliation for their complaining about sexual harassment. There is also the chance of blackmail—an employee showing an interest in you, hoping you will grab the bait so she or he can accuse you of sexual harassment.

If you find yourself becoming attracted to a subordinate, remember the words of former Secretary of State Henry Kissinger when he was asked why a rather average-looking man like himself was able to attract gorgeous women: "Power is the ultimate aphrodisiac." What he meant was, if he were a nobody, gorgeous women would have no interest in him. Only because he held a position of power were they interested.

What does this have to do with sexual harassment? Plenty. You have probably heard the cliché, "Sexual harassment isn't about sex, it's about power." Kissinger proved that that cliché is half true: Sexual harassment is about power. But it is also about sex. In fact, it is usually more about sex than about power.

When a male boss expresses a sexual interest in a female subordinate, the boss is not just showing off his power. (For the purpose of this explanation, I will use the example of a male boss and a female subordinate, but it could just as easily be the other way around.) He is thinking about sex, not power. His power, however, might make certain things happen. It might make him a bit more confident that the subordinate will accept his invitation for a date. It might also make the subordinate more interested in the boss, not because she fears the consequences of turning him down, but because she genuinely finds him more attractive than she would if he had no "power."

Women will sometimes flirt with or be interested in a man who is their boss yet would not be interested in him if he were of equal rank to them. They are attracted to his "power" more than they are attracted to him, really. Not that they are looking for anything in return. They are not necessarily looking for a raise or promotion or job security. They are simply intrigued by the thought of dating a man with "power," just as men are intrigued by dating women with power.

This dynamic is indeed gender-neutral. Men are sexually attracted to powerful women just as women are sexually attracted to powerful men. Power is, as Kissinger said, the ultimate aphrodisiac regardless of which gender holds the power. Men are often attracted to women executives and women politicians who would not be so attractive to these men if these women were waitresses and sales clerks. These men are also attracted to waitresses and sales clerks, but a waitress or sales clerk might have to be more physically attractive than a woman executive or politician to arouse sexual interest in these men. Some women probably think that women with power are a turnoff to men. Maybe some men are turned off by them, but many men are attracted to them, just as many women are attracted to men with power.

So if you are a male boss and you think the attraction between you and a female subordinate is mutual, ask yourself this question: If you were not her boss, would she be attracted to you? If your answer is no, do not attempt to romance her. She is intrigued by your power, and is possibly, though not necessarily, trying to get ahead in your company. A male subordinate might try to do the same with a female boss. There is usually no legal problem if that subordinate does get ahead in your company. But if that subordinate does not get ahead in your company, that subordinate will blame you and might sue you and your company for sexual harassment. Do not succumb to temptation without thinking through all the ramifications.

If you are quite certain that the subordinate is genuinely interested in you and would be even if you were not his or her boss, then nonetheless tread very carefully. It is legally unwise to date a subordinate, but if you really want to, try to make sure that the attraction is mutual and has nothing to do with the power you have over her. If she has given you no hint whatsoever that she is interested in you, don't ask her out.

If you do ask out a subordinate and she says no, or she gives you some lame excuse ("Uh, I have company coming in this weekend"), don't ask again. Forget about it. If it doesn't happen easily, give up. Don't be persistent in trying to get a date with a subordinate. You are asking for trouble. If she or he turns you down or gives you an excuse, don't pout or walk off in a huff. Any anger or frustration you exhibit will be noticed and can be used against you by that subordinate if you ever have to fire, demote, or take some other type of adverse employment action against her. She will say it is because she turned you down for a date.

What about dating co-workers, that is, people of the same rank as you? That is usually okay. Just remember, though, the higher up you are in the company, the fewer the employees you can safely attempt to romance.

Should your company adopt a no-dating rule, that is, a rule that says no employee can date a co-employee? Or a rule requiring the two employees (or just the subordinate employee) to sign a form indicating that the relationship is totally consensual? There is rarely a good reason for such rules, but it might depend on the circumstances.

If an employee complains to you that she is being bothered by or pursued too aggressively by a co-worker and asks you to intercede and tell the pursuer to stop, do so. Whenever you receive a complaint that someone is being sexually harassed, ask the victim what she wants you to do about it. If she is unsure, tell her there is little or nothing you can do about it—other than reminding all your employees of your sexual harassment policy—until she decides what she wants you to do about it. Don't be afraid to tell her to first try to work the problem out herself with the harasser. The harasser will usually be angrier if the victim goes over his head or behind his back (that is, complains to the harasser's boss or to other people in the company) than if the victim complains to the harasser directly. Nearly all men will stop harassing a woman once the woman makes absolutely clear to him that she is not interested in him. The problem is when the woman gives mixed signals or has already had a lengthy, intimate relationship with the man. It then becomes more difficult to persuade the man that "no means no." Be patient, however. If the harassment victim needs your assistance to formulate a plan to deal with the problem (such as when she is being harassed by a supervisor), assist her.

Should your company adopt a policy strictly prohibiting supervisors and executives from dating subordinates? That is a tough call. Such a policy reduces the risk of sexual harassment lawsuits but might not be good human resource management. The opportunity for romance is an important—though unofficial—employee "benefit." A company where unmarried men and women have opportunities to find romance will attract more and better job applicants and have better employee morale than a company that prohibits such opportunities.

I emphasize the word "unmarried," however. Extramarital romance is a morale buster, not booster. A married boss dating an unmarried (or married) subordinate, or an unmarried boss dating a married subordinate, will offend most employees who witness it or know about it. It will also offend most jurors. Juries are more likely to "award" a sexual harassment victim big damages if the harasser was married than if the harasser was unmarried. In a jury's view, an unmarried supervisor is free to at least try to get a date or establish a romantic relationship with a subordinate—not to be too persistent about it, but to at least ask once. A married supervisor is not free in this regard.

Sexually Hostile Work Environment

"Sexually hostile work environment" refers to sexual advances, sexual conduct, or sexual comments that are so severe or so repetitious that they make it more difficult for the victim to do her job. They must be that offensive in order to be legally classified as "sexual harassment," at least under federal law and the laws of nearly every state. And they must be "unwelcome." If the boss was not aware of the employee's displeasure with the conduct or comments, and the employee did nothing to make him aware (she didn't tell him and she didn't tell any other person of authority), and the conduct, comments, or advances were not that bad, she will probably lose.

Frequently people ask whether one sort of conduct or another comprises sexual harassment. "If I look at my secretary's legs, is that sexual harassment?" "My boss told me a dirty joke; is that sexual harassment?" "Our top customer, a "macho man," keeps asking our saleswoman for a date, and he always hugs her and puts his arm around her. Can she claim sexual harassment?" (This is called "third-party sexual harassment.") "Our sales clerk objects to our selling Playboy on the magazine rack; she claims it is sexual harassment." "Is it sexual harassment if one of our guys has the Sports Illustrated swimsuit calendar over his desk, or displays a picture of his girlfriend in a string bikini?"

The answer is usually no. If that is all that happened—one little incident or a few little incidents—that is not sexual harassment. To be sexual harassment, the conditions have to be severe or repetitious. Grabbing a female employee's breast is severe. If it happens once, she might have a case. But the less severe the conduct, the more repetitious it has to be to amount to sexual harassment. If the conduct was not repetitious or severe, but the subordinate nonetheless complained about it and asked you to put a stop to it, and you did not put a stop to it, it may or may not be sexual harassment. It would depend on the circumstances.

Sexual objects, sexual jokes, sexual e-mail, sexual humor via Internet, sexy calendars, very sexy photographs of boyfriends, girlfriends, or strangers, and very sexual innuendoes might, if severe or repetitious enough, comprise sexual harassment.

Also, it is usually a good idea not to allow employees to wear clothing that is too revealing. Such clothing invites jokes and sexual harassment.

Miscellaneous Types of Sexual Harassment

As mentioned before, there are some other types of sexual harassment: "third-party sexual harassment" and "sexual favoritism." Third-party sexual harassment occurs when an employee complains that someone associated with the company but not an employee of the company is sexually harassing the employee. For example, a waitress complains that a drunk customer is sexually harassing her. Employers who serve a lot of alcohol are probably more likely to be sued for "third-party" sexual harassment than those who do not.

There have been few third-party sexual harassment suits. That is because few victims of third-party sexual harassment get fired for complaining about it. A customer cannot fire your employee.

Sexual favoritism occurs when employee A is given a raise or promotion, or is retained rather than terminated in a company downsizing, because she or he is having some kind of sexual or romantic relationship with the boss. Employee B, who has the same job title and boss but is not given a raise or promotion, or is terminated in the downsizing, sues for sex discrimination. Employee B claims that employee B was discriminated against "because of sex." The law is not entirely clear on whether employee B has a case, but if employee B can prove that employee B was at least as good as, or better than, employee A, then employee B may well have a case. Sexual favoritism is a form of sexual harassment or sex discrimination.

Use your common sense and do not engage in or tolerate such types of harassment/discrimination. If you must tell your biggest customer to stop harassing your saleswoman, do so (as gently and diplomatically as possible, of course).

Sexual harassment is illegal even if the harasser is harassing someone of his or her own sex. It is illegal for a man to sexually harass a man, and it is illegal for a woman to sexually harass a woman.

Sexual Harassment Prevention Training is Required in Many Workplaces

Connecticut has a regulation that mandates companies with 50 or more employees to provide two hours of sexual harassment prevention training and education to all supervisors. Other states might have a similar requirement.

Should You Fire the Sexual Harasser?

Asking me if you should fire the sexual harasser is like asking me if you should fire the manager who discriminates against women in hiring, promotion, and other terms and conditions of employment. Sexual harassment is a form of sex discrimination. Should you fire the manager? Or should you give the manager a stern warning but not fire him? I cannot answer that question in this book. It depends on the circumstances.

If you automatically fire an employee because someone accused him of sexual harassment, you run the risk that the harasser will sue you for wrongful termination, especially if the accusation was false or exaggerated. So be careful. Investigate. Ascertain if the accusation is true. Firing an innocent man could cause him to sue you. Whether he would win the suit depends on circumstances. It is like firing an employee who you think stole money from your company but who in fact did not. If he is an employee at will, you have the right to fire him for any reason, no reason, or even a mistaken reason. However, firing an employee for a mistaken reason often leads the employee to believe that that was not the real reason you fired him. It often leads him to believe that you had a discriminatory reason. It often leads him to believe that you would not have fired him had he been a different race, gender, religion, age, sexual orientation, or other protected classification. Firing an employee for a mistaken reason may also weigh on your conscience.

Forgiveness (that is, giving the sexual harasser a warning but not firing him) may be "godly," but lawsuits are costly. So I cannot answer the question "Should your fire the sexual harasser?" You must answer it yourself, depending on circumstances.

Keep in mind that many men who were fired or forced to resign because they sexually harassed an employee were otherwise good employees. It is hard to replace good employees. An employee of a public school system alleged that her supervisor, a popular school administrator, sexually harassed her. The school system fired the administrator. Parents were disturbed to learn he sexually harassed an employee, but they were also disturbed to learn he (the administrator) was fired. Talented employees are hard to replace. Ask yourself whether your company will be better off with him or without him.

Chapter 5

Prevent Religion Discrimination

If you know, or think, an employee or job applicant's religious beliefs are different from yours, and you are contemplating firing, demoting, denying a promotion to, or not hiring this employee or job applicant, ask yourself: What if this employee or applicant's religious beliefs were different than they are? (You might also ask yourself what if this employee or applicant's religious beliefs were the same as yours, but I am somewhat hesitant to suggest doing so, because some people discriminate against people of their own religion.) Would you be taking such action? If your answer is yes, then you can probably fire, demote, not promote, or not hire this employee or applicant. If your answer is no, then don't take such action. If your answer is no, it means religious differences are influencing your thinking.

Employers cannot discriminate against employees because of religion. Employers cannot segregate employees because of religion, such as assigning an employee to a non-customer contact position because of actual or feared customer preference. Federal law (Title VII of the Civil rights Act of 1964) defines "religion" to include "all aspects of religious observance and practice as well as belief." Religion includes not only traditional, organized religions such as Christianity, Judaism, Islam, Hinduism, and Buddhism, but also religious beliefs that are new, uncommon, not part of a formal church or sect, only subscribed to by a small number of people, or that seem illogical or unreasonable to others. A belief is "religious" for Title VII purposes if it is "'religious' in the person's own scheme of things," i.e., it is a sincere and meaningful belief that occupies in a person a place parallel to that filled by God.

Religious beliefs include theistic beliefs as well as non-theistic moral or ethical beliefs as to what is right and wrong which are sincerely held with the strength of traditional religious views. Although courts generally resolve doubts about particular beliefs in favor of finding that they are religious, beliefs are not protected merely because they are strongly held. Rather, religion typically concerns "ultimate ideas" about "life, purpose, and death." Social, political, or economic philosophies, as well as mere personal preferences, are not "religious" beliefs protected by Title VII.

Religious observances or practices include, for example, attending worship services, praying, wearing religious garb or symbols, displaying religious objects, adhering to certain dietary rules, or refraining from certain activities. Determining whether a practice is "religious" depends not on the nature of the activity, but on the employee's motivation. The same practice might be engaged in by one person for religious reasons and by another person for purely secular reasons. Whether or not the practice is "religious" is therefore a situational, case-by-case inquiry. For example, one employee might observe certain dietary restrictions for religious reasons while another employee adheres to the same dietary restrictions but for secular (e.g., health or environmental) reasons. In that instance, the same practice might in one case be subject to reasonable accommodation under Title VII because an employee engages in the practice for religious reasons, and in another case might not be subject to reasonable accommodation because the practice is engaged in for secular reasons. The Equal Employment Opportunity Commission (EEOC) gives the following example:

> Sylvia wears several tattoos and has recently had her nose and eyebrows pierced. A newly hired manager implements a dress code that requires that employees have no visible piercings or tattoos. Sylvia says that her tattoos and piercings are religious because they reflect her belief in body art as self-expression and should be accommodated. However, the evidence demonstrates that her tattoos and piercings are not related to any religious belief system. For example, they do not function as a symbol of any religious belief, and do not relate to any "ultimate concerns" such as life, purpose, death, humanity's place in the universe, or right and wrong, and they are not part of a moral or ethical belief system. Therefore, her belief is a personal preference that is not religious in nature.

In addition to, or related to, the duty not to discriminate on the basis of religion, the law imposes on employers a duty to "reasonably accommodate" their employees' religious practices. If a Muslim woman wants to cover up her body so that only her face, hands, and feet are showing—as may be required by her religion—you probably have to allow her to do so even if it conflicts with your dress code or uniform, although it might depend on whether her religious attire (burqa, hijab, or other) poses a health or safety risk to her or others. If a Jewish employee needs to leave work at 5:00 p.m. on Friday to attend religious services or to take Saturday off completely, you probably have to allow him to. Whether you must allow him to depends on how much of a hardship it would be to you (or to your company) if he left at 5:00 p.m. Friday or took Saturday off. If a Sikh employee wants to wear a beard, you might have to allow him to.

EEOC takes the position that discrimination against atheists is religious discrimination and therefore is illegal.

You may have the right to inquire whether an employee who seeks a religious accommodation is really a follower of that religion. Some employees suddenly claim to follow a religion just so they can take a few days off or work reduced hours. If you have reason to believe that an employee who is asking you for a religion accommodation is faking his religion or exaggerating some religious requirement, you can require him to provide documentation that he really is a follower of that religion and that the religion really does have that requirement. But be careful. If you require Jews and Muslims to prove they are Jewish or Muslim but don't require Christians to prove they are Christian, that might be illegal discrimination.

What about your religious rights as a business owner or manager? Do you have the right to display Christmas decorations? What if a non-Christian complains about them? Would you have to take the decorations down? Can you forbid Christmas decorations? Can you offer Bible-study sessions? Can you require employees to attend them? Can you display the Ten Commandments at work? Can you require employees to attend church? Can you invite employees to attend church with you?

It is difficult to answer these questions in a short book such as this. The answer might be very different if you are a government employer than if you are a private-sector employer.

Some general words of caution are in order, however. First, there is a difference between religious decorations and religious services. There are few if any cases in which a private-sector employer has been sued (and lost) for displaying religious decorations. If an employee were to complain, you might have to take down the decorations that are in that employee's immediate work area. If employees of other religions wish to display their own religious decorations at their own workstations, you probably have to let them.

As for religious services (prayer services), you probably have the right to offer them but not the right to compel employees to attend. You cannot punish or discriminate against employees who do not attend. And keep this in mind: Employers who conduct or offer prayer services in the workplace are almost inviting employee lawsuits even if the employees have little chance of winning these suits. If an employee is fired, not promoted, or not hired, he or she will likely claim to be a victim of religious discrimination. He or she will claim that the employer prefers to hire, promote, and retain people of a certain religion. Employers who conduct or offer religious activities in the workplace probably do prefer employees who are of the employer's religion. While it is legal to express your religious views, it is illegal to discriminate against employees because their religious views differ from yours. So be careful. Be especially careful if the religion your company or organization espouses is not a mainstream religion. A jury might be less likely to sympathize with your company or organization.

If your company or organization serves a particular religious purpose (for example, if it is a church, synagogue, or mosque), the rules are somewhat different. Only members of your religion may be qualified to hold certain jobs. Religion may be a bona fide occupational qualification (BFOQ) for certain jobs. But other jobs can be held by members of any religion, and you do not have the right to discriminate on the basis of religion when hiring, promoting, and retaining people for these other jobs.

Chapter 6

Prevent Disability Discrimination

"Make level paths for your feet, so that what is
lame may not be dislocated, but rather be healed."

Hebrews 12:13

The laws prohibiting race discrimination, sex
discrimination, religion discrimination, and sexual
orientation discrimination are based on the assumption
that race, sex, religion, and sexual orientation do not
affect job performance. The laws prohibiting disability
discrimination, on the other hand, are based on the
assumption that some disabilities affect job
performance but others don't. Some disabilities make
job performance very difficult or impossible. It is
illegal to discriminate against an employee because he
has a disability, but, on the other hand, it is ordinarily
(there might be an occasional exception to this) legal,
not illegal, to discriminate against an employee if his or
her job performance is not as good ("able") as that of
your other employees. To some people, that might
sound like doubletalk. It might sound like a Catch-22.
An employee has to be disabled to claim disability
discrimination, but if his disability makes him do his
job poorly, the employer can terminate him for doing
his job poorly. But it actually makes sense. Let me
explain.

The Law Protects Employees Who Can Do the Job, or Can Do the Job with Reasonable Accommodation

If an employee has a disability but it does not affect his or her job performance, or affects it in a minor way, an employer cannot terminate him for having such disability. So if you are contemplating terminating such an employee, ask yourself: "Would I be firing this disabled employee if he or she were not disabled?" If your answer is yes—you would be firing the employee if he or she were not disabled—you can, ordinarily (except in some unusual circumstances), fire the employee and not be held liable for disability discrimination (and hopefully not even get sued).

However, some disabilities do affect job performance. Some disabilities make it very difficult or impossible to perform certain jobs. That is why they are called disabilities. If the disability makes the person unable to do the job, you generally do not have to hire or retain that person, but before you make a decision about that you must first consider whether some inexpensive mechanism or "accommodation" exists which would enable the person to do the job as well as your other employees do. If such a "reasonable accommodation" exists, you must provide it. You must provide it unless providing it would cause you undue hardship.

Disability discrimination law assumes that (1) not all disabilities affect job performance, (2) a particular disability might affect the job performance of some employees who have that disability but not other employees who have that disability, and (3) even if a disability does make it difficult or impossible for an employee to do the job, there may exist some type of inexpensive mechanism or accommodation that enables that employee to do the job as well as the employer's "abled" (the opposite of disabled) employees do. Consequently, if there exists such a mechanism or accommodation, the employer is required to provide it. If there does not exist such a mechanism or accommodation and the disabled employee simply cannot perform the job as well as the employer's "abled" employees do, the employer need not hire or retain that disabled employee.

In other words, disability discrimination law protects people who can do the job. Those who cannot do the job even with whatever mechanisms or accommodations are reasonably available are not protected by the disability discrimination laws. You do not have to hire or retain them.

Thus, employers should not have a stereotypical view of disabilities. For example, an employer should not assume, just because an employee suffers from depression (which is usually a "disability" under the Americans with Disabilities Act, or ADA), that the employee's job performance will be less than that of employees who do not suffer from depression. It might or might not be less. With most disabilities, employers should look at the disabled employee as an individual who may or may not have the same work problems as someone else with that disability.

Here are the general principles of disability discrimination law: If an employee's disability prevents the employee from performing the essential functions of the job in accordance with your company's standards (that is, prevents him from performing them as well as your "abled" employees perform them), you can terminate him; however, you first must consider whether there exists some mechanism or accommodation that might enable him to perform up to those standards. If such a mechanism or accommodation exists and you can provide it without undue hardship (financial or other type of hardship) to your company, you must provide it.

You can require the employee to pay that part of the cost of the accommodation that is an undue hardship to your company. However, you must first try to determine whether tax credits or deductions might offset the cost of the accommodation, and also explore whether funding might be available from an outside source, such as a state rehabilitation agency.

These requirements are called reasonable accommodation. If no reasonably affordable mechanism or accommodation exists that will enable the employee to perform up to your company's standards, then you need not hire or retain that employee. For example, if your company requires all its clerical people to be able to type at least 70 words per minute accurately, and a disabled employee or job applicant cannot type more than 50 words per minute accurately even with whatever accommodations or mechanisms could reasonably be provided to him or her, you need not hire or retain that employee/job applicant.

The important point to remember is that you do not have to tolerate lesser productivity from a disabled employee than you do from an employee with no disability. You can tolerate lesser productivity if you want to, but you don't have to. Disabled employees can be held to the same standards as abled workers. An employer need not evaluate disabled employees by a lower standard. However, you do have to explore whether a lesser-performing disabled employee might be able to perform as well as your abled employees if he or she is provided with some type of reasonably inexpensive mechanism or accommodation.

You have to be careful in the job-interviewing process not to ask employees if they have disabilities or to question them about disabilities. You can tell them what the various aspects of the job are and you can ask them if they can perform the various aspects of the job and to demonstrate that they can. Asking them to submit to a medical examination or to provide medical documentation is sometimes permitted in the hiring process. There is an EEOC regulation promulgated under the federal Rehabilitation Act of 1973 that took effect in 2014. It requires many government contractors to "invite," but not require, job applicants with disabilities to identify themselves as such. It is "affirmative action" to help people with disabilities land jobs. But as I understand the regulation, such self-identification should be kept separate from the job application itself and from the people interviewing the applicant. This is fairly new and developing at this writing (January 1, 2018), so talk to your lawyer and/or read the regulation for details.

Asking current employees (as opposed to job applicants) to submit to a medical examination is permitted if job related and consistent with business necessity.

What types of accommodations might you have to provide a disabled employee to enable him or her to perform the essential functions of a particular job in accordance with company standards? There are manuals on this topic and thus no need to list them all here. Most are a matter of common sense. One accommodation you may have to provide is sick time and light duty. You may have to provide extra sick days (in most cases, the extra sick days can be unpaid), light duty, a leave of absence, or some scheduling flexibility to an employee to accommodate his or her disability. At some point, however, if the employee is absent too much, the employee will no longer be considered a "qualified individual" under the disability discrimination laws. In essence, he will no longer be regarded as "qualified" for the job, and thus can be legally terminated.

Disability discrimination law can be rather tricky and difficult to explain in a short book and, like all types of discrimination, the answers to specific questions often depend on which state you are in. Generally speaking, though, common sense and decency will suffice to keep employers out of trouble and cost them very little or nothing. Employers can easily comply with the disability discrimination laws without giving up anything in productivity or discipline.

A good way to understand an employer's duty to reasonably accommodate an employee's disability is by thinking of the Biblical passage, "Make level paths for your feet, so that what is lame may not be dislocated, but rather be healed" (Hebrews 12:13). Although you might not have the ability to "heal" (cure or eliminate) an employee's disability, you do have the ability and obligation to make a "level path" for the employee. You should provide a workplace in which disabilities pose as little a problem for the disabled employee as possible. "Level paths" can mean, literally, ramps and aisles that are handicap-accessible, and can also mean other accommodations.

"Disability" Defined

The legal definition of disability under the Americans with Disabilities Act ("ADA") is rather vague: "a physical or mental impairment that substantially limits one or more of the major life activities of [the employee]." "Major life activities" include, for example, caring for oneself, performing manual tasks, seeing, hearing, eating, sleeping, walking, standing, lifting, bending, speaking, breathing, learning, reading, concentrating, thinking, communicating, and working. "Major life activities" also include the operation of a major bodily function, for example, functions of the immune system, normal cell growth, digestive, bowel, bladder, neurological, brain, respiratory, circulatory, endocrine, and reproductive functions. In 2011 Congress and the EEOC made it easier for employees to establish they have a disability. Congress passed the ADA Amendments Act of 2008 (ADAAA). The EEOC issued regulations interpreting the ADAAA. The EEOC declared:

> The primary purpose of the ADAAA is to make it easier for people with disabilities to obtain protection under the ADA. Consistent with the Amendments Act's purpose of reinstating a broad scope of protection under the ADA, the definition of "disability" in this part shall be construed broadly in favor of expansive coverage to the maximum extent permitted by the terms of the ADA. The primary object of attention in cases brought under the ADA should be whether covered entities have complied with their obligations and whether discrimination has occurred, not whether the individual meets the definition of disability. The question of whether an individual meets the definition of disability under this part should not demand extensive analysis.

....

For example, ... it should easily be concluded that the following types of impairments will, at a minimum, substantially limit the major life activities indicated: Deafness substantially limits hearing; blindness substantially limits seeing; an intellectual disability (formerly termed mental retardation) substantially limits brain function; partially or completely missing limbs or mobility impairments requiring the use of a wheelchair substantially limit musculoskeletal function; autism substantially limits brain function; cancer substantially limits normal cell growth; cerebral palsy substantially limits brain function; diabetes substantially limits endocrine function; epilepsy substantially limits neurological function; Human Immunodeficiency Virus (HIV) infection substantially limits immune function; multiple sclerosis substantially limits neurological function; muscular dystrophy substantially limits neurological function; and major depressive disorder, bipolar disorder, post-traumatic stress disorder, obsessive compulsive disorder, and schizophrenia substantially limit brain function. The types of impairments described in this section may substantially limit additional major life activities not explicitly listed above. [29 Code of Federal Regulations section 1630].

In other words, EEOC goes on to say, "disability" includes, for example (these are just examples) deafness, blindness, intellectual disability (formerly known as mental retardation), partially or completely missing limbs, mobility impairments requiring use of a wheelchair, autism, cancer, cerebral palsy, diabetes, epilepsy, HIV infection, multiple sclerosis, muscular dystrophy, major depressive disorder, bipolar disorder, post-traumatic stress disorder, obsessive-compulsive disorder, schizophrenia, any mental or psychological disorder, organic brain syndrome, emotional or mental illness, and specific learning disabilities."

But this 2011 development should not alarm employers. Many millions of employees in the U.S. can prove they have some type of disability, according to the ADAAA and EEOC. This does not necessarily mean they can win a disability discrimination lawsuit. It merely means that the employer's focus should be on whether the employer is complying with the law rather than on whether the employee qualifies as being "disabled." Courts rarely require employers to put up with a disabled employee's job performance if that job performance falls short of the job performance of the other employees (the employees who have no disability), so long as the employer makes a reasonable effort to help the employee perform up to the standards set for employees who have no disability. Just having a disability doesn't get an employee very far in a disability discrimination lawsuit. The employee must also prove discrimination or failure to reasonably accommodate a disability. Failure to reasonably accommodate a disability is a form of disability discrimination, according to the ADA.

Put another way, the mere fact that an employee is disabled does not help him win an ADA lawsuit any more than the fact that an employee is black helps him (the black employee) win a race discrimination lawsuit. The key question, as to the black employee, should be not whether he is black but whether the employer is discriminating against him because he is black. Likewise, the key question as to the disabled employee should be whether the employer is discriminating against him because of his disability (or failing to reasonably accommodate the disability).

An employee also has a "disability" under the ADA if he has a "record of such an impairment" or is "regarded as having such an impairment." For example, an employee who was committed to a mental hospital 10 years ago might be "regarded" by some people as still mentally impaired today even if he has a "clean bill of health" today. He also has a "record of such an impairment."

Short-term illnesses and short-term injuries (minor illnesses and injuries lasting or expected to last less than six months) are usually not "disabilities" under the ADA, though it might depend on circumstances. Pregnancy is not a "disability" (it is not an "impairment"), but certain impairments resulting from pregnancy (e.g., gestational diabetes) may be considered a disability if they substantially limit a major life activity, and Connecticut now requires employers to reasonably accommodate pregnancy in a way similar to how employers must accommodate disability. I discussed this new Connecticut law (it took effect on Oct. 1, 2017) in detail in chapter 3 (Prevent Sex Discrimination).

I encourage you to become familiar with the U.S. Equal Employment Opportunity Commission's website and the website of your state agency that has jurisdiction over employment discrimination claims. The EEOC's website, in particular, has a lot of helpful information, including information pertinent to specific disabilities such as cancer, diabetes, deafness (and other hearing impairments), blindness (and other vision impairments), and other disabilities, and also information pertinent to some specific types of employers, such as restaurants, other food service providers, and some other specific types of employers.

If an employee claims to have a condition that is a disability and asks that you accommodate it, and you are not sure whether the employee really does have that condition, ordinarily you have the right to ask the employee to furnish medical proof that he has this condition. This is particularly true of non-obvious ("invisible") disabilities such as mental disabilities, headaches, depression, learning disabilities, certain types of back pain, and other disabilities that an employee can fake or exaggerate. Just because an employee claims he has one of these conditions does not mean the employer has to take the employee's word for it. The employer can ask the employee to produce medical records to show he has this condition. If the employee refuses to produce the records or if the records do not indicate that he has this condition, the employee must somehow prove to the employer that he has the condition. If he doesn't, the employer need not provide the accommodation. Disability, like religion, is often invisible. That means it can be faked or exaggerated. Employers have a right to ascertain whether the employee is faking or exaggerating it.

Chapter 7

Prevent Age Discrimination

In the United States in general (there are exceptions depending on the size, location, and type of employer), it is illegal to discriminate against an employee because of his or her age if he or she is 40 or older. In other words, generally speaking in the U.S., it is illegal to discriminate against older workers (40 or older) because of their age but not illegal to discriminate against younger workers because of their age. Connecticut state employment discrimination law does not specify the age of 40. Connecticut state law seems to provide that it is illegal to discriminate against anyone on the basis of age, so long as the person is old enough (16 years old, 18 years old, or what the minimum age is) to work that job. There is debate in Connecticut and perhaps some other states over whether an employee must be at least 40 years old to sue for age discrimination. Rather than focus on this debate, I suggest the following.

If you (the employer or manager) are, say, 45 years old and are contemplating firing a 60 year-old employee, ask yourself: "Would I be firing this employee if he were 30 years old?" Even if you yourself are 60 years old (or older), you should, in this mental exercise, use 30 years of age rather than your own age because some people think that people their own age (and even a few years younger) are "too old" for a particular job. There are 60 year-old executives who think a 60 year-old is "too old" for some jobs.

Many people misunderstand age discrimination law. They think age discrimination law makes it illegal to terminate older workers. Or they think employers have to allow older workers to slow down and be less productive than younger workers.

They are mistaken. Older workers can be terminated just as younger workers can. If an older worker is unable to perform the job as well as all your younger workers do, you can terminate him. This is true even if his inability is due to the effects of aging. You are thereby terminating him not because of age, but because of job performance.

If, on the other hand, he is able to perform the job as well as your younger workers, you must treat him no differently than you treat them.

That is not only what the law says, it is what the Bible says. "Honor the elders. Let the elders who rule well be counted worthy of double honor" (1 Timothy 5:17). "Likewise you younger people, submit yourselves to your elders" (1 Peter 5:5). So if an elderly employee is "ruling well," or performing well, don't fire her just because she is elderly. But if she is not performing well, you need not "honor" her with continued employment.

Years ago, many companies had a mandatory retirement age. Today, in regard to most (not all, but most) job categories, it is illegal to have a mandatory retirement age. That is, in regard to most job categories, it is illegal for an employer to require an employee to retire at a certain age. There are some exceptions. It is legal for an employer to require highly paid executives and policymakers with good pension plans to retire at 65. It is legal to require some public safety officers, such as police officers and the military, to retire at a certain age, and legal to restrict new hires for public safety officers to people under a certain age.

In regard to most job categories, the law requires you to make an assumption: that age, if 40 or older (but in Connecticut and perhaps a few other states, any age that is old enough to be hired for the job), has no effect on job performance. But obviously that assumption is not always correct. Some workers, especially in highly physical job categories, become less effective at their jobs as they get older. For example, in January 2018 there is no one, to my knowledge (perhaps I'm mistaken) over the age of 45 playing in the National Football League, Major League Baseball, the National Basketball Association, or the National Hockey League. Only a handful are over 40. Hundreds of major-league athletes in their early 40s are "cut from the team" (terminated) each year and replaced with younger athletes. The diminished ability of the older athletes is due to the effects of aging and the general wear and tear that eventually takes a toll on a major-league athlete.

If older athletes are cut from the team due to their diminished ability, does that mean they are victims of age discrimination? No. They were terminated not because of age but because of job performance. True, their job performance declined due to age. But they were terminated due to job performance, not age. If a 22 year-old were performing no better than these 42 year-olds, he would be terminated, too.

That is what I mean when I say age discrimination law is about assumptions. Remember what I said about sex discrimination: don't assume, just because a 150-pound person is female, that she cannot perform a job as well as a 150-pound man. Maybe she can, maybe she can't. Don't make assumptions just because she is female and he is male. Get the facts. It may well be that that particular woman cannot perform the job as well as that particular man. But don't just assume it because she is female.

So too with age discrimination. Don't assume, just because an employee is older, that he is unable to perform as well as younger employees perform. Don't assume that older workers ("older" being defined in federal age discrimination law and in most states' age discrimination laws as 40 or older) are physically or mentally slower, more apt to retire, or more apt to get sick or die soon, than younger workers are. Some are, some aren't. Ordinarily (there might be an occasional exception to this), you should not ask an employee if, or when, the employee plans to retire, unless the employee mentions it first, and even then you should try to focus the discussion on the employee's plans, not the employee's age.

However, if for whatever reason, including age, an employee cannot perform as well as your younger employees perform, you need not retain that employee. As with handicap discrimination law, if age has caused the employee to be less effective than your other employees, you can terminate that employee. You can terminate an employee for being less effective than your other employees. So focus on job performance and ignore age. That is easy in baseball because baseball performance is easily measured in numbers. The speed of a pitcher's fastball is easily measured by a machine. A batter's job performance is easily measured by familiar (to baseball fans) statistics such as batting average, home runs, and runs batted in. But in most other types of jobs, performance is not so easily measured. When performance is difficult to measure, managers are more apt to consider age.

Managers should not do that. Managers should ignore age. How do you ignore age? Easy. When contemplating terminating an older worker, pretend the worker has a full head of hair (and the same color hair the employee had when young), unwrinkled skin, and all other outward appearances of youth. Pretend you have no idea how old the worker is. Then ask yourself: "Is this worker performing as well as my younger workers?" If he or she is not—in other words, if his or her job performance is worse than that of all your younger workers in the same job category and perhaps some similar job categories—you can terminate this older worker. But if even one younger worker is a worse performer than the older (40 or older) worker, reconsider whom to terminate. Perhaps you should terminate the younger one, or maybe both of them.

Suppose you have a 62-year-old job applicant. Ignore his age. Focus solely on his qualifications. Pretend he is 32 years old. If a 32-year-old with the same qualifications applied for the job, would you hire the 32-year-old? If your answer is no, you do not have to hire the 62-year-old. If your answer is yes, you should probably hire the 62 year old. Your answer is based solely on qualifications, not age.

Here is a little song, or rhyme, you can keep in mind to help you understand and comply with age discrimination law. It is sung to the tune of "This Old Man":

> This old man,
> He can sue;
> I'll pretend he's thirty-two.

In other words, if you are contemplating terminating an older worker, pretend that a 32 year-old worker (a worker who is 32 and looks 32) were performing the job with the same speed and effectiveness that this older worker is performing it. Would you fire the 32 year-old? If your answer is yes—you would fire the 32 year-old worker—then you can probably fire the older worker. If your answer is no—you would not fire the 32 year-old—then don't fire the older worker. If your answer is no, it means that the employee's age, not his job performance, is influencing your thinking. When his age, not job performance, is influencing your thinking, that is age discrimination and is generally illegal.

Having a workplace that reflects the age of the general population (or is above the age of the general population) reduces your likelihood of being accused of age discrimination.

Tips to Help Prevent Becoming a Victim of Age Discrimination

What can older workers do to prevent being discriminated against? Three things: exercise, education, and mentoring. Exercise enables older workers to stay in good physical shape and avoid getting overweight. Physically fit older workers are far less likely to be discriminated against than physically unfit ones are. You don't have to dye your hair or tattoo your body. You can "look your age." But try to look as good for your age as you possibly can. Make your skills, not your age, stand out.

Older workers should consider taking college courses and other continuing education courses. This demonstrates their willingness and ability to learn and change. It is sad to read about older workers being downsized out of jobs they have held for many years. But whose fault is it? Is it the fault of the employer, or is it the fault of the employee? Some employees get complacent as they get older, do not maintain their skills and good attitude, and do not learn new skills. When they get fired, they think it is because of their age. Sometimes they are right. But more often it is because they got complacent, did not maintain their skills and good attitude, and did not learn new skills. In those situations, the firing is not age discrimination. Such employees would have been fired if they were 32 years old.

Older workers should mentor younger workers and help younger workers succeed. If you help a younger worker and she later becomes a CEO, and you need a job someday, maybe she will return the favor and hire you.

One problem for many older workers is they become too dependent on one employer—their employer. If that employer terminates them, they are devastated. They fear they will not be able to find a job elsewhere at their age. But again, whose fault is that? The employer's? Or their own? Employees should maintain employability, so that if an employer fires them or lays them off, they can go out and find another job without too much difficulty. Employers should encourage employees to maintain employability. Employers should encourage employees to maintain their skills, learn new skills, and learn new technology. Getting dumped by an employer is like getting dumped by a girlfriend or boyfriend: Painful though it is, the pain goes away as soon as the dumped one finds another (satisfactory) girlfriend or boyfriend. An employee who quickly finds another job is less likely to sue you than one who suffers a long period of unemployment.

Note that I use a boyfriend or girlfriend analogy, not a marriage analogy. Some employees are as devastated by losing a job as they would be if their spouse died or divorced them. They have no right to feel this way. They were not "married" to the employer. Few, if any, of them had a lifetime contract with the employer, as husbands and wives have with each other. They were, in most cases, employees-at-will, meaning they had the right to quit at any time without explanation, and the employer had the right to terminate them at any time without explanation so long as the employer was not motivated by the employee's race, color, national origin, sex, or other illegal reason. They should simply move on and find a new employer. Employers should help them prepare for this possibility by encouraging them to keep themselves in good vocational shape so they are attractive to other employers.

Here is a story that illustrates the point.

The Parable of the Boyfriends and the Girlfriends

Two men had attractive girlfriends ("girlfriend" and "boyfriend" are acceptable words to refer to romantic companions even if the "girl" and "boy" are both well over 18; this is an exception to the "rule" that says men should not refer to women over 18 as "girls"). The first man got complacent about the relationship and gained 50 pounds of flab. When his girlfriend dumped him without explanation, he felt hurt. But the hurt intensified when he found that he was unable, due to being so out of shape, to land another attractive woman. So he kept trying to win back the girlfriend, which made him (and her) even more miserable. He became a nuisance to her.

The second man also got dumped without explanation, but he had stayed strong and fit, so he easily found another attractive woman to date and quickly forgot about the woman who dumped him. In fact, the woman who dumped him eventually got jealous and tried to win him back, without success.

The moral of the story is, an employee who stays "in shape" is less likely to bother (sue) an employer if the employer "dumps" (fires) him. He'll find another job easily. This is true even if he is an older employee. Although some employers discriminate against older employees, many do not. Many prefer older employees.

So encourage your employees to stay in good vocational "shape." If you eventually fire them or lay them off, they will find new jobs quickly and be less likely to try to drag you down with them. Furthermore, you might just decide not to fire them or lay them off. An "in shape" employee is one you won't want to lose!

Chapter 8

Prevent Sexual Orientation Discrimination

Sexual orientation discrimination violates the state law of Connecticut and at least 20 other states. Whether it violates the federal law (Title VII of the Civil Rights Act of 1964) is unclear. If it violates the federal law, it is illegal in all 50 states for employers with 15 or more employees. The question under Title VII is whether discrimination against an individual because of sexual orientation is discrimination "because of sex." If it is, it violates Title VII. Many people do not believe that such discrimination is "because of sex." They believe that discrimination "because of sex" means refusing to hire women, or refusing to hire men, or paying women less than men, or something like that. To them, discrimination because of the sex of the employee's sex partner is not discrimination against an employee "because of sex." I cannot predict how the Supreme Court will rule on this if the Court rules on it. In Connecticut, New York, and Vermont, the U.S. Court of Appeals for the Second Circuit may rule on the question sometime in 2018. I cannot predict how that court will rule. I cannot predict whether Congress will amend Title VII to clarify whether sexual "orientation" discrimination is "because of sex."

Because sexual orientation discrimination is illegal in Connecticut, where I live and practice law, and approximately 20 other states, I will write this chapter as though sexual orientation discrimination is illegal throughout the United States. If you feel strongly about whether sexual orientation should or should not be illegal, don't just wait and see what happens. Express your opinion. Make your voice heard. Urge your lawmakers to do what you think is right.

If you know, or think, an employee is gay, lesbian, or bisexual, and you are contemplating firing or demoting this employee, ask yourself: What if this employee were heterosexual? Would you be taking such action? If your answer is yes, then you can probably fire or demote this employee. If your answer is no, don't take such action.

From a lawsuit prevention standpoint, it is better that you not know who is gay and who is not. If you do not know, and you do not think, an employee is gay, it will be difficult for the employee to accuse you of sexual orientation discrimination. Therefore, don't ask about it. Don't tell about it. Don't talk about it. Don't think about it. Just ignore the sexual orientation of your employees. The less you know about their sexual orientation, the better. It is possible that someone might criticize you for ignoring, rather than "celebrating," diversity, but sometimes you have to ask yourself: Do I want to celebrate diversity, or do I want to prevent lawsuits? Sometimes you must choose between the two.

Some of you might feel that laws protecting gays from discrimination in the workplace conflict with the Bible. The Bible forbids homosexuality (Leviticus 18:22; 20:13; 1 Corinthians 6:9; Romans 1:26-27), yet these laws protect homosexuals from discrimination in the workplace. There is no conflict. These laws do not require you to approve of homosexuality. They require you not to discriminate against employees for being homosexual. In other words, these laws permit you to disapprove, in your heart and mind, of homosexuality, but do not permit you to play God. The law is the same as stated in the Catechism of the Catholic Church, which requires acceptance of homosexuals but does not require approval of homosexuality. "They must be accepted with respect, compassion, and sensitivity. Every sign of unjust discrimination in their regard should be avoided" (Catechism, paragraph 2358).

Does this mean I am in favor of same-sex marriage? No. It doesn't mean I am in favor of it, and it doesn't mean I am against it. Catechism paragraph 2358 says unjust discrimination should be avoided. It does not say that all discrimination should be avoided. Remember what I said early in this book: Not all discrimination is unjust. The marriage laws serve a different purpose than the employment laws. The employment laws protect the right to earn a living. The marriage laws reward two people for staying together. Should the law reward two men for staying together? In 2015 the Supreme Court (in Obergefell v. Hodges) held that it should. Do I agree? This book is about employment, not marriage, so I will express no opinion about it in this book.

Some employees who sue for sexual orientation discrimination are not gay, lesbian, or bisexual. They are, or claim to be, heterosexual. What are they suing for, then? They are suing based on what is called "perceived" homosexuality. The boss referred to the employee by using a word or name—derogatory or neutral—that means or implies that the employee is gay, lesbian, or bisexual. In some states, if an employee is fired or otherwise treated less favorably because the employer believed or perceived him or her to be gay, lesbian, or bisexual, or somehow identified him or her as gay, lesbian, or bisexual, the employee can sue for sexual orientation discrimination even if the employee is not gay, lesbian, or bisexual.

Many people refer to the lesbian, gay, and bisexual community as the LGBT community. "T" stands for "transgender." "Transgender" includes, for example, men who dress like women and wear women's makeup and lipstick, and includes people who undergo sex-change operations. Can an employer fire a male employee because he wears a dress or skirt to work, or because he underwent a sex-change operation and now looks and sounds, or tries to look and sound, like a woman? In Connecticut and some other states, the answer is no.

The Bible (Deuteronomy 22:5) says, "The woman shall not wear that which pertaineth unto a man, neither shall a man put on a woman's garment: for all that do so are abomination unto the Lord thy God." Note that the biblical rule for women is not identical to the biblical rule for men. It says the woman shall not wear what "pertaineth" unto a man. It does not say,

107

"The woman shall not put on a man's garment." By contrast, it says a man shall not "put on a woman's garment." I read that to mean that according to the Bible, a woman can wear pants but a man cannot wear a dress. That is just my opinion. Does the law conflict with the Bible? Decide for yourself.

Is an employer required to refer to an employee by the gender the employee chooses, or may the employer refer to the employee by the gender the employee was at birth? Managerial employees of the federal government during the latter years of the Obama administration were, I believe, required to call an employee by the pronoun the employee chose to be called. Whether that is true in the Trump administration, I cannot say with certainty. Different supervisors may have different policies depending on the employee. Some state governments may require it. Ask a lawyer in your state.

What about employers with contracts with the state (for example, Connecticut) or federal government? Are they required to use the pronoun the employee chooses? As of today (January 1, 2018), I do not know the answer to this. I'm not sure there is a clear answer to this. In 2014 President Obama issued Executive Order 13672, which prohibits federal contractors from discriminating against employees on the basis of sexual orientation or gender identity. It adds sexual orientation and gender identity to the prohibited bases of discrimination in Executive Order 11246, which is the familiar affirmative action order for federal contractors that has been in effect for many years. The Office of Federal Contract Compliance Programs (OFCCP) has promulgated rules for contractors to comply with Executive Order 13672. Read them if they pertain to your company. Some transgender rights advocates assert that employers must now call an employee the pronoun the employee chooses. I don't know whether they are asserting that the law requires it, or they are just advocating for it. Consult a lawyer in your state.

If an employee who has always been male while in your employ announces he is transitioning, or has transitioned, to female, and wants to use the women's restroom and be called "she" and "her," must you grant the employee's request? Can you ask the employee if the employee still has a penis? If the employee still has a penis, can you deny the employee's request? Consult a lawyer in your state.

If an employee who was a man now claims to be a woman, most transgender rights advocates are opposed to the employer's asking the employee to prove it. Most transgender rights advocates don't want employers to focus on "what's in trans people's pants," reported the June 9, 2014, Time magazine (p. 43, in an article entitled "America's Transition"). Such focus is "maddening for us," said Mara Keisling, executive director of the National Center for Transgender Equality in the Time article. "It's just not what any of us thinks is an exceptionally interesting thing about us," Keisling said. I am guessing (perhaps I am mistaken) that many of your female employees will be angry if a person with a penis is allowed to use the ladies' room. Whether you must allow a person with a penis to use the ladies' room, I will not discuss any further in this book. Talk to a lawyer in your state for advice in such a situation.

Three years ago (2015) I attended a wedding (this particular wedding was between a man and woman) and happened to be seated at the same dinner table as a friend of mine who is a urologist. Everyone at the table knew he is a urologist. Someone asked him what, exactly, is sex-change surgery. In this brief conversation—it was brief because it is not the type of conversation that most guests at a wedding want to hear—here is what I think the urologist said. I am not certain I heard him correctly, so don't rely on what I am saying here. Ask a urologist yourself if you want information about this. I think he said that many—not all, but many—men who have had "sex-change surgery" and now want to be regarded as female still have a penis.

To me, a person with a penis is a male. And even if he cuts off his penis, that does not make him a female, in my view. "God created man in His own image . . . male and female" (Genesis 1:27). It takes a male and female to conceive a child. In my opinion, a male cannot truly become a female, and a female cannot truly become a male. I am not a scientist or medical doctor. I am merely telling you my personal opinion. You may have a different opinion. Why God created two sexes, and what each person should do with

110

his or her sexual anatomy, I will not opine about in this book. This book is about human resource management.

I am extremely reluctant to call someone a pronoun (he, she, him, her) other than the one he or she was at birth. I will do so only if the law forces me to. St. Peter said, "Submit yourselves to every ordinance of man for the Lord's sake" (1 Peter 2:13). That means you should obey the law, but it does not mean you must accept the law as final and unchangeable. All laws can be changed. That is, all laws created by humans—as distinguished from God's law—can be changed by humans. If you don't like a law, you can become politically active and try to change the law. If you don't like the Supreme Court's decision on same-sex marriage (Obergefell v. Hodges), you can become politically active and urge passage of a federal constitutional amendment to overrule Obergefell v. Hodges. You can urge President Trump to appoint justices to the Supreme Court who would overrule the Obergefell case. If you like the Obergefell v. Hodges decision, you can oppose efforts to overrule it.

Congress is presently (2018) controlled by Republicans. Republicans are more inclined to call an employee the pronoun the employee was at birth.

I personally do not classify people as "straight," "heterosexual," "homosexual," "gay," "lesbian," "bisexual," or "transgender." I classify people as "male" or "female." A male has a penis. A female has a vagina. I am not a scientist or medical doctor. I'm just telling you my personal opinion, for what it's worth.

The employer's defense in a sexual orientation discrimination suit is often, "I had no idea he is gay. I fired him because of his poor job performance, not his sexual orientation. I didn't know what his sexual orientation is." If the employer is telling the truth, it will be very difficult for the employee to win the suit. If the employee never indicated to the employer what the employee's sexual orientation is, the employee will have difficulty proving that the employer "knew" or "perceived" the employee to be gay, lesbian, or bisexual. If the employer did not know or perceive it, the employer could not possibly have discriminated against the employee on the basis of it.

For that reason, diversity training pertaining to sexual orientation is inadvisable. That type of diversity training makes almost everyone feel uncomfortable. It generates discussion about a topic that many people have strong feelings about but would rather not discuss in the workplace. Negative feelings, if expressed, can be used against them and against the company in court. The more interest and curiosity you show in an employee's sexual orientation (some diversity trainers urge managers to show such interest in their employees), the more legal trouble you potentially bring upon yourself and your company or organization. A gay, lesbian, or bisexual employee might accuse you of prying into his or her love life because you are "homophobic" and you are trying to "get rid of" homosexual employees. Keep in mind that you cannot please everybody. If an employee or diversity trainer is displeased because you do not want to talk about sexual orientation in the workplace, keep in mind that your first obligation is to comply with the law. In the approximately 20 states that prohibit sexual orientation discrimination in the workplace, the best way to comply with the law is to ignore the sexual orientation of your employees.

Suppose you disapprove of homosexuality. Can you express your disapproval to your employees? My answer to that question is basically the same as the answer I gave previously in this book about a somewhat related topic: religion. You probably have the right to politely (that is, not in a harassing or threatening way) express your disapproval of homosexuality to your employees, but if you do, you significantly increase the risk, if you fire an employee who is gay, lesbian, or bisexual, of being accused of sexual orientation discrimination. Thus, you have rights, including the First Amendment right of freedom of speech to express your views, but your employees also have rights, including the right not to be discriminated against or harassed on the basis of sexual orientation. Sometimes rights clash, and it is difficult to predict whether a court will balance those rights in your favor or in your employee's favor. The safest legal advice in the approximately 20 states that prohibit sexual orientation discrimination is to ignore your employees' sexual orientation and not express your disapproval (if any) of homosexuality to your employees.

Avoid Labels ("Gay," "Straight," etc.) as Much as Possible

Although I do not classify people as "straight," "heterosexual," "homosexual," "gay," "lesbian," "bisexual," or "transgender," I occasionally use those words. I use them because you probably use them. I use them to communicate with you. But I have a suggestion. I suggest we all stop using those words. I suggest we not label people that way, even in our minds. Those labels are nebulous. They do not distinguish between sexual urges and sexual acts. Some people have homosexual urges but do not act on those urges. They engage in heterosexual sex or no sex. Are they gay? Those labels do not distinguish between past, present, and future. If a man was married to a woman for 10 years, divorced her, and is now in a homosexual relationship, is he gay? Bi? If a man was in a series of homosexual relationships but is now in a heterosexual relationship, what label is he? Straight? Ex-gay? Those labels do not distinguish between the sex organ and other parts of the body. If a man is sexually aroused thinking about muscular men but has never touched, nor desired to touch, another man's penis and never kissed, nor desired to kiss, a man's mouth, is he gay? If he marries a muscular woman, is he trying to cover up his homosexual tendencies? If a woman is married to a delicate, effeminate man, is she lesbian? Is he transgender? I suggest that everyone stop using those labels. I try to use only two labels—"male" and "female"—and I use them only to the extent I believe is necessary and warranted in the circumstances.

114

Chapter 9

Prevent Discriminatory Language

"By your words you will be justified, and by your words you will be condemned."

Matthew 12:37

Eliminate from your vocabulary, especially your workplace vocabulary, all offensive words that pertain to race, color, ethnicity, ancestry, national origin, sex, pregnancy, religion, old age, physical or mental disability, and sexual orientation. If a jury hears that you uttered discriminatory slurs, the jury might conclude that you committed employment discrimination even if you did not. Also, such words might constitute racial harassment, ethnicity harassment, national origin harassment, sex/gender/sexual harassment, age harassment, disability harassment, genetics harassment, or sexual orientation harassment. Harassment based on one or more of those categories is a form of discrimination based on one or more of those categories. Here is a story that illustrates the point.

The Parable of the Latino Factory Worker

A Latino male (we'll refer to him as "the client") went to a lawyer complaining that the client's boss, Mr. Smith—a gruff, white, semi-educated factory owner—

used an ethnic slur to refer to Latinos and fired him for being late too often. Although the client was indeed late too often, he wanted to sue for race discrimination or ethnicity discrimination. He felt that if a white employee had been late that often, Smith would have given the white employee one more chance to improve his punctuality, rather than fire him.

The lawyer asked the client how many of Smith's 100 employees are Latino. The client replied 50. The lawyer advised the client that he (the client) might have a good race discrimination case or ethnicity discrimination case, and suggested in passing that he go to work for the competing factory a mile away.

The competing factory was owned by Mr. Jones, a dignified white man with an Ivy League education who is on many civic boards, goes to church every Sunday, and never utters a slur of any type. The client's reply to the lawyer's suggestion was, "I don't think I can get a job there. Jones does not hire Latinos. He does not like Latinos. So I want to sue Smith to get my job back."

Who's the bigot, Smith or Jones? Ordinarily, actions speak louder than words. Smith's actions show him to be an equal opportunity employer—half of his employees are Latino. Jones has no Latino employees (or he has a few "tokens" just to avoid being accused of having an all-white workforce). Jones is the bigot. Smith might be somewhat bigoted, but Jones is a worse bigot.

But who does the client wish to sue? Smith! Why? Because Smith used an ethnic slur and fired him. He does not wish to sue Jones even though Jones is more bigoted than Smith and even though Jones would have refused to hire the client at all. In employment discrimination law, words often speak louder than actions.

That is the sad irony of employment discrimination law. Most of the suits are initiated by people who were fired, not by rejected job applicants. Yet the people who were fired usually aren't the ones who were discriminated against. The rejected job applicants—the people who weren't hired to begin with—are more likely to be the ones who were discriminated against. Yet they are less likely to sue.

Jones will probably get sued eventually. An employer should not try to avoid discrimination suits by simply refusing to hire women, people of color, older workers, and disabled workers. That is illegal. But that isn't the point here. The point here is that some of the most fair-minded employers—the ones who hire the most women and people of color—end up getting sued because they make offensive, discriminatory remarks. Don't make such remarks! Discriminatory remarks can get an employer into trouble even if the employer has a good or even excellent record of hiring women, people of color, older workers, and disabled workers.

Remember also that some people who would never utter a discriminatory slur under ordinary circumstances might do so in extraordinary circumstances, such as when they are extremely agitated. Maybe you are one of them. A white worker, in a heated argument with a black co-worker, yells a racial epithet at the black co-worker. Or a young worker will call an older worker an "old" this or that. Or a male manager will call a female employee a gender-specific slur. Make a conscious effort to "catch yourself" when you're angry, so you do not utter such slurs.

And don't allow any other employee of yours—even your lowest-level employee—to make such remarks in the workplace. Such remarks create a discriminatorily hostile work environment.

I considered making a list of all these discriminatory slurs, or as many as I could think of, and including the list in this book so you would know all the words to avoid. Some people do not know that all these words are offensive. But the list would be too offensive to put in the book. So the book leaves out the really bad words (words that everyone, or almost everyone, knows are racial slurs, gender slurs, or other discriminatory slurs) and mentions a few that you might not realize can get you into legal trouble.

Never refer to an employee as "crazy," "nuts," "wacko," "paranoid," or "schizoid," even if he or she is. Discrimination against an employee because of mental disability can sometimes land you in legal trouble; so can harassment because of mental disability (or physical disability). You can talk to your fellow managers about, or discipline or discharge an employee for, the employee's poor job performance, but do so

118

using nondiagnostic language. Don't "diagnose" the employee yourself unless you are a psychiatrist. If you suspect that the employee is mentally unfit, you may have the right to ask the employee to submit to a mental examination. You may, depending on how bad the employee's behavior or job performance is, have the right to terminate the employee without a mental examination. But don't play psychiatrist. If anyone is going to make a mental diagnosis, let it be a psychiatrist or other qualified mental health professional.

Never, ever, tell an employee that he or she is "too old," unless it is for a job for which the law prohibits employment of people over a certain age. Don't even tell someone else that an employee is "too old." Don't say "old fart," "old fogey," "old geezer," "geezer," "dinosaur," or any other words meaning or implying old age. Don't say "We need younger people around here" or "We need new blood in this department." If you need personnel changes in a department, say "We need personnel changes in this department." You can terminate older employees just as you can terminate younger employees, but don't do it just because they are old, and certainly don't tell them they are old. Don't ever say "He's a good young marketing manager." An older worker will take offense at that, might make a note of it, and might use it against you someday in an age discrimination suit.

Don't refer to any racial, ethnic, or religious group as "you people." Don't say "you women!" or "you men!" In other words, don't lump people together just because they belong to a particular racial, ethnic, religious, or gender group. If a Jewish employee orders a ham sandwich for lunch, don't say, "I thought Jews don't eat pork." Some Jews do, others don't. Don't talk about an employee's religion unless the employee brings it up, in which case you should still try to politely stay away from the topic (except that you may need to discuss it if the employee is asking for some type of religious accommodation, such as leaving by 5:00 on Fridays, not working Sundays, etc.).

If you are a man, don't refer to a female over the age of 18 as a "girl." She is a "woman." Don't say "the girls in the office." Say "the women in the office" or, better yet, "the people in the office." Don't say "PMS," "that time of the month again," or any other words or phrases pertaining to menstruation.

If you are a woman, particularly a woman supervisor, don't say things that might lead a man to sue for sex discrimination. For example, don't say "It's their male culture" or "That's a guy thing" or "There's too much testosterone in this department."

Employers who say anything negative about homosexuality, heterosexuality, or bisexuality run the risk of being accused of sexual orientation discrimination. I discussed this in the previous chapter.

Language that is particularly offensive to members of a certain race, color, ethnicity, national origin, sex, religion, age (especially if over 40), physical or mental disability, or sexual orientation can get you into legal trouble. It can and will be used against you in court if an employee ever sues you for discrimination. It may even be the basis for the suit. It may be the only evidence the employee has. But it may be enough for the employee to win. Don't use such language even if you are in the same classification as the person you are talking to or about. For example, don't use language that is offensive to blacks, even if you are black.

Have a Written Policy Prohibiting Discriminatory Slurs and Discriminatory Harassment, and Distribute It to All Employees

It is a good idea for employers to have a written policy distributed to employees that prohibits harassment, slurs, and other adverse behavior based on race, color, ethnicity, national origin, ancestry, sex, sexual orientation, pregnancy, age, religion, and disability. The policy will inform all your employees what type of behavior is unacceptable. Having such a policy might shield your company or organization from liability for punitive damages if your company or organization is ever held liable for discrimination or harassment. In some cases, it might shield your company or organization from liability altogether.

Should you have a policy that bans all forms of harassment (a "No Harassment of Any Kind" policy), not just discriminatory or unlawful harassment? The problem with a "No Harassment of Any Kind" policy is that some employees feel "harassed" anytime the employer tries to get the employee to work harder or better. If an employee is constantly late to work, and you are constantly warning the employee that tardiness could lead to the employee's dismissal, the employee might feel that you are "harassing" him or her, especially if, in the opinion of the employee, the employee feels that he or she has a good excuse for being late. To some employees, any effort by a supervisor to counsel an employee, warn an employee, or improve an employee's job performance is "harassment." Thus, the line between "harassment" and "supervision" is not always clear. Even if the counseling does not amount to "harassment," an employee might think it is harassment. Thus, having a "No Harassment of Any Kind" policy might make your managers afraid to discipline an employee. Managers might fear they will be accused of "harassing" the employee. Suffice it to say that supervisors should not engage in any type of discriminatory (or illegal) harassment. Also, some states are contemplating passing laws prohibiting any and all harassment or "bullying" in the workplace, so keep an eye on legislative developments regarding harassment and bullying.

Chapter 10

Some Tips to Reduce Damages and Lawyers' Fees

So much of human resource management these days is based on fear of lawsuits and fear of lawyers fees that I want to offer some of my thoughts and tips on how employers can reduce those costs. If an employee sues a company, the company has to pay the company's lawyer or law firm to defend the company in the lawsuit, and if the employee wins the suit, the employer will also be required to pay the employee and might also be required to pay the employee's lawyer or law firm.

As an employer, you should try to keep your legal expenses low. But what do I mean by "legal expenses?" Do I just mean the money your company pays your company's lawyer or law firm? No, that is not all I mean. The money your company pays to your company's lawyer can possibly (but not necessarily) be kept low simply by hiring an inexpensive lawyer. Is that a good idea? Maybe, maybe not. It is possible that your company might save money on lawyer fees, but your company might (or, then again, might not) lose money in other ways if the inexpensive lawyer is not as knowledgeable or skillful as a more expensive lawyer.

So, should you hire a high-priced lawyer? Most high-priced lawyers are very good lawyers but they are also very good at making money. High-priced lawyers who represent employers make most of their money from the employers. The employers (companies) pay substantial fees or salaries to their lawyers (fees to their outside law firms, salaries to their in-house lawyers if they have in-house lawyers). With some (not all, but some) high-priced lawyers, even if the lawyer's advice is good, the lawyer's fees are high to a point where the employer ends up with less money than if the employer had hired a lower-priced lawyer. It is also important to keep in mind that the "price" of legal services is sometimes difficult to measure. One reason is that a law firm that charges $500 per hour might be able to handle a case by doing 50 hours of work (total fee: $25,000), while a law firm that charges $300 per hour might do 100 hours of work (total fee: $30,000) to achieve the same result. Which is the more expensive firm? It is debatable. Of course, it is also possible that the law firm that charges $500 per hour will do 100 hours of work in the case (total fee: $50,000), while the $300-per-hour law firm might do 50 hours of work (total fee: $15,000) to achieve the same result. One problem with evaluating lawyer fees is that you never know what the result would have been had you hired a different lawyer. You don't know what the lawyer's fee would have been, and you don't know what the result of the case would have been.

In my view, a company's "legal expenses" in employment law consist of (approximately) eight items: 1) the money the company pays the lawyer or law firm who advises and represents the company in employment law; 2) the money the company pays, in the form of "damages," to employees (and in some cases, to the employees' lawyers) who sue the company or threaten to sue the company, 3) the money the company pays to employees in the form of severance packages in exchange for the employees' signing a waiver (sometimes called a "release") that waives (or "releases") their right to sue the company; 4) the money the company throws away in wages and salaries to employees that the company would like to fire but is afraid to fire due to the company's fear of lawsuits; 5) the money the company pays to human resources (HR) managers and other managers to document employee mistakes and poor job performance (one can argue that this documentation serves the purpose of trying to improve the employee's job performance, but in many companies the main reason they do all this documentation is to defend themselves if an employee sues the company or threatens to sue the company); 6) the lost productivity that results when employees, who think the company is afraid to fire them due to the company's fear of lawsuits, do not work as hard or as well as they are capable of working; 7) the money the company pays to the government in fines and other expenses if the company violates a labor law or employment law; and 8) if the company purchases employment practices liability insurance, the money the company spends to purchase that insurance. Maybe there are additional items I have not thought of, but those eight are the ones that come to my mind. With some law firms, the law firm is good at helping you keep one or more of these eight items low but you realize no savings from it because their advice to you causes the other items to be high. In my opinion, and this is just my opinion (perhaps others would disagree), the ideal law firm is the one that helps you keep the sum total of items (1), (2), (3), (4), (5), (6), (7), and (8) as low as possible. That is what I think law firms should try to do. Keeping the sum total of these eight items as low as possible should be the goal of law firms, employers, and society as a whole. Hopefully, the suggestions I have made in this book will help employers lower the sum total of those eight items.

In Some States, Seek Damage Caps

I have another suggestion. If you are an employer in Connecticut, Massachusetts, or one of the other states that has an employment discrimination law (a state law) that enables, or possibly enables, an employee to collect higher damages in an employment discrimination lawsuit than the federal laws do, consider doing this: Ask your state senator, state representative, and/or governor to put a maximum limit of $50,000 to $300,000, depending on how many employees your company or organization has, on the amount of money a court can force a company or organization to pay an employee for "emotional distress" and "punitive" damages in an employment discrimination lawsuit in your state. If your company has fewer than 15 employees, consider asking for a maximum limit on "emotional distress" and "punitive" damages lower than $50,000 (say, $20,000). Such maximum limits (called caps, or damage caps) exist under most (not all, but most) of the federal employment discrimination laws, but the federal employment discrimination laws allow each state, if a state so chooses, to "award" (force an employer to pay an employee) higher damages than the federal law allows. Under federal employment discrimination law, an employee who wins a discrimination lawsuit can collect from the employer the amount of money the employee lost as a result of the discrimination, plus an amount of money for emotional distress and punitive damages. Except in race discrimination lawsuits, where there is no cap on damages, the amount for emotional distress and punitive damages is capped at $50,000 if the employer has 15 to 100 employees, $100,000 if the employer has 101 to 200 employees, $200,000 if the employer has 201-500 employees, and $300,000 if the employer has more than 500 employees [42 United States Code, section 1981a(b)(3)].

Massachusetts (Mass. General Laws chapter 151B, § 9), Connecticut (Conn. General Statutes § 46a-104), and some other states have no caps. Suppose a very small employer in Massachusetts, say, an employer with only 8 employees, decides to terminate an employee. Let's say the employee was making $12 per hour ($24,000 per year). If the employee sues for discrimination, and a jury decides the employer should be compelled to pay the employee a million dollars, the employer might have to pay the employee a million dollars. If the employer doesn't have a million dollars, the employer might have to declare bankruptcy. By contrast, a small employer (8 employees) in a state that has damage caps (as described in the above paragraph) would have to pay as follows. Let us assume that the employee is out of work for one year after being fired, then lands another job paying $12 per hour. The employer would have to pay the employee $24,000 (the amount of money the employee lost as a result of the discrimination), plus a maximum of (no more than) $20,000 for emotional distress. That is a total—and maximum—of $44,000. Plus, the employer would have to pay the employee's lawyer's fees. So, with damage caps, the maximum total is probably (there may be an occasional exception to this) between $60,000 and $80,000. Without damage caps, the sky is the limit. If the jury says the employer should pay the employee a million dollars, the employer might have to pay the employee a million dollars. If an employer hires someone in Connecticut or Massachusetts, and then for some reason fires that employee, the employee can, with a good lawyer and a sympathetic jury, possibly bankrupt the employer. In states with damage caps, the damages more accurately reflect the economics of the business: A small employer would not have to pay a huge sum of money.

In 2016 the Connecticut Supreme Court in Tomick v. United Parcel Service, Inc., ruled that punitive damages are not available under Conn. General Statutes § 46a-104. Does that mean that damages for emotional distress are unavailable? I don't think the answer is clear. So even after the Tomick case, it may behoove Connecticut employers to try to persuade the

Connecticut legislature to amend § 46a-104 and declare that emotional distress damages are either unavailable or capped by the same amounts as the federal caps.

Putting a cap on damages would almost certainly reduce the number of employment discrimination lawsuits. Why? Because many employees would not sue if the most they could collect were $50,000 (or even $100,000, $200,000, or $300,000) plus their lost wages and attorney's fees. Many sue only if they have a chance of winning millions or many hundreds of thousands of dollars. They sue the way they buy lottery tickets: They don't buy a ticket if the prize is "only" $50,000 but will wait in line all day and buy 20 tickets when the prize is $50 million. The odds against winning $50 million are astronomical, and nearly everyone could benefit from winning "only" $50,000, yet they don't enter the "game" if the prize is "only" $50,000. These people enter only if they can win millions or many hundreds of thousands of dollars. Many employees who sue employers think that way. They have a lottery mentality.

Damages in defamation suits and some other types of employee lawsuits would still have no cap in many states. Maybe your state legislature would be willing to impose caps in all employee lawsuits, but I don't know.

If these states, including Massachusetts and Connecticut, were to impose this cap on emotional distress damages and punitive damages in employment discrimination lawsuits, employers in these states would no longer have to worry that a court might order them to pay millions of dollars in emotional distress damages and/or punitive damages in such a lawsuit. Even if a jury were to "award" (ask the court to force the employer to pay) such a large amount, the judge would be required by law to reduce the emotional-distress and punitive components of the "award" to $300,000 if the employer has 500 or more employees, $200,000 if the employer has 201-500 employees, $100,000 if the employer has 101-200 employees, $50,000 if the employer has 15-100 employees, and less than $50,000 if the employer has fewer than 15 employees.

Because the potential damages in these cases would be considerably lower, settlement amounts would be considerably lower too. Why settle a case for $500,000 if the most you can lose at trial is $200,000? Likewise, lawyer fees would be lower. A law firm will have difficulty charging an employer $100,000 to defend against an employment discrimination lawsuit if the most the employer can lose in the lawsuit is $50,000. Also, employers feel compelled to spend far more for "preventive" legal services if damages are uncapped than if damages are capped.

Outrageously high jury verdicts are rare, but they can happen in any case, and thus have the effect of scaring employers in many states into thinking they must spend vast sums of money to settle cases and prevent future cases. Frankly, I believe this is one reason why some employers move jobs from the northeastern states (where there are no damage caps) to the southern and western states (where there are damage caps). If the employer ever terminates an employee and an employee sues, the suit will be less expensive if there are damage caps.

Another way to address this problem (the problem of uncapped damages for emotional distress and punitive damages in Connecticut, Massachusetts, and some other states) is to ask Congress to pass a law declaring that no state's employment discrimination law can provide higher damage awards than are allowed under the analogous federal law. Whether Congress would be willing to pass such a law, I don't know. You may want to write to your Congressperson, U.S. Senator, and/or the President about this.

I am not a lobbyist. I am just trying to help employers reduce their costs. Over the past 39 years, I have seen employers in Connecticut, Massachusetts, and some other states spend huge sums of money on lawyers, trainers, and human resources (HR) consultants due to the employers' enormous fear of employment lawsuits. This enormous fear drives many HR decisions. Many employees are allowed to be mediocre and unproductive because their bosses are afraid to fire them, due to the potential cost of such a lawsuit. This book hopefully will help employers reduce the number of, and cost of, these lawsuits. One way this book does so is by teaching employers how to prevent discrimination in the first place. Another way is

131

to point out to employers that they can try to get their lawmakers to put a cap on emotional-distress damages and punitive damages in state-law employment discrimination lawsuits.

If someone tells you that a cap on damages in employment discrimination lawsuits would be unconstitutional or invalid in any way, ask them the basis of their assertion. Ask them exactly why they think such a cap would be unconstitutional or invalid. What section of state law, the state constitution, federal law, or the federal (U.S.) Constitution would be violated? Courts in some states have held caps on damages in personal injury lawsuits (lawsuits in which someone was physically injured) unconstitutional because personal injury law is, for the most part, a "common law tort" which has traditionally been decided, as to liability and damages, by juries, but I am not aware of any courts holding caps on damages in employment discrimination lawsuits unconstitutional. Employment discrimination lawsuits are statutory (not "common law"), so legislatures have the authority to put limits on them.

Alternative Dispute Resolution (ADR)

St. Paul said, "Do not sue the Brethren . . . . It is already an utter failure for you that you go to law against one another" (1 Corinthians 6:1-7). He said, "Avoid foolish disputes, genealogies, contentions, and strivings about the law; for they are unprofitable and useless" (Titus 3:9). Can justice be achieved without lawsuits?

132

Lawyers call it "alternative dispute resolution" (ADR). What is ADR? What is it an "alternative" to? Is it something new? Or is it old wine in a new flask?

According to Cornell University Law School's Legal Information Institute (LII), ADR is "any method of resolving disputes other than by litigation," or "any means of settling disputes outside of the courtroom." LII says:

> ADR typically includes early neutral evaluation, negotiation, conciliation, mediation, and arbitration. As burgeoning court queues, rising costs of litigation, and time delays continue to plague litigants, more states have begun experimenting with ADR programs. Some of these programs are voluntary; others are mandatory.

LII defines "litigation" as "the process of resolving disputes by filing or answering a complaint through the public court system." So, "ADR" is the process of resolving disputes by filing or answering a complaint through private channels rather than the public court system.

Does ADR reduce damages and lawyer fees? I honestly don't know. Consider this scenario. Joe works for XYZ Company. XYZ Company has been told that ADR is a good way to reduce damages and lawyers fees in employment discrimination cases. So XYZ Company requires all its new employees to sign an agreement that says any dispute between the employee and XYZ Company will be resolved by arbitration, not litigation. If an employee refuses to sign it, that employee cannot work at XYZ Company. Is it legal for XYZ Company to do this? Ordinarily, yes. There might be some exceptions to this, but generally speaking it is legal. Generally speaking, such an agreement is enforceable. Talk to a lawyer about any specific situation.

Joe signs the agreement and begins work at XYZ Company. Three years later, XYZ Company fires him. He thinks he was fired discriminatorily, that is, because of his race, sex, age, religion, or other category discussed in this book. Can he sue XYZ Company for discrimination? The answer is semantic. What does it mean to "sue?" As I will demonstrate to you, it makes little or no difference what it means to "sue." The fact of the matter is, regardless of whether Joe can "sue," Joe can, if he proves to the arbitrator that XYZ Company violated the discrimination laws, collect as much money from XYZ Company as he could if he were allowed to sue in court, and XYZ Company will have to spend a lot of money in lawyer fees to represent XYZ Company in the arbitration. Joe can also file a complaint with EEOC (U.S. Equal Employment Opportunity Commission) or the fair employment practices agency of his state (Connecticut, Texas, or other state).

The main differences between arbitration and litigation (the word "litigation" usually means a lawsuit filed in court or a complaint filed in some other type of governmental agency) are 1) arbitration usually takes place in a building that isn't called a "courthouse," 2) the arbitrator—the person who will decide whether the employer violated the discrimination law and, if the arbitrator decides the employer did violate the discrimination law, how much money the employer should be required to pay the employee—is usually a private citizen wearing a business suit rather than a government employee wearing a black robe (the government employee wearing a black robe is called a "judge"; the arbitrator is called an "arbitrator"), 3) there is no "jury" (6 or 12 neutral citizens) in arbitration (the arbitrator is both the judge and jury), and 4) it is usually very difficult to appeal an arbitrator's decision, although I must say it is usually difficult to appeal a judge's decision or jury's verdict in litigation. Perhaps XYZ Company will have to pay somewhat less to XYZ Company's law firm to handle the arbitration than XYZ Company would have to pay the law firm to handle a similar case in litigation, but I don't know how much less. There is usually less "discovery" (depositions, interrogatories, and documents) in arbitration than in litigation. The trial, if the case goes to trial, is usually shorter in arbitration than in litigation. The trial will usually occur sooner in arbitration than in litigation. The dispute will be more "public," and therefore possibly more embarrassing, in court than in arbitration.

But these "savings" can cut both ways. They make it faster, cheaper, and less embarrassing for the employer, but they also make it faster, cheaper, and less embarrassing for the employee. Many employees are more worried about being embarrassed in court than employers are. In many, if not most, discrimination cases, the employer is critical of the employee's job performance. The employer will often testify about the errors or omissions the employee made which led the employer to terminate him. If the suit is in court and therefore open to public scrutiny, many people might learn what the employer is saying about the employee's job performance. The employee might look more foolish than the employer. It is the employee, not the employer, who has to go find another job. An employee who looks foolish in a court case might have more difficulty landing another job than an employee who either goes to arbitration or does not make a claim to begin with. Such an employee might therefore prefer arbitration to litigation.

Accordingly, I believe (some lawyers might disagree with me on this) that an arbitration agreement between an employer and employee ("ADR") might actually increase, rather than decrease, the number of discrimination claims. I believe (perhaps I'm mistaken) that the faster and easier it is for an employee to present a claim of discrimination, get it decided, and collect money from the employer, the more likely the employee is make a claim of discrimination.

Some employers, and some lawyers, believe that arbitrators tend to award employees less money than juries do, but I am not aware of any reliable data to support that belief. There might be some reliable data, but I am not aware of it.

Furthermore, I believe that it is easier for one person (an arbitrator) to be unfair to an employer than it is for seven people (a judge and six-person jury) to be unfair to an employer. To win in arbitration, the employee usually must persuade only one person—the arbitrator—unless there is more than one arbitrator. To win a jury trial in many states, the employee must persuade at least 80% of the jurors. So, although it may (or may not; I am not sure) be true than the average juror is more sympathetic to employees than to employers, the fact remains that the employee must persuade more than a mere majority of the jurors. The employee usually must persuade at least 80% of the jurors, and sometimes must persuade all the jurors.

Some employers might be clever and want to insert a clause in the arbitration agreement that limits the arbitrator's award to no more than, say, $50,000. That might sound like a good way to reduce damages and lawyers fees. But some courts have held that an arbitration agreement that limits damages in an employment discrimination case to an amount lower than the employee would be entitled to in court is void in that regard. Such a "liquidated damages" clause might be valid in other types of disputes but not in employment discrimination disputes.

Be careful if and when you read about the dollar amount of "average jury awards" in employment discrimination lawsuits. Some people (perhaps not many people, but some people) might be trying to scare you into choosing arbitration (or other "ADR") over litigation, or into choosing expensive training programs to prevent discrimination lawsuits. Ask questions such as: How was the "average" computed? Does the "average" include all the jury verdicts in employment discrimination lawsuits in a particular state or region, or does it include only the jury verdicts the person who calculated the "average" has read or heard about? Does the "average" include all the jury verdicts that were in favor of the employer (if the jury found that the employer did not violate the discrimination laws, the jury award was zero), or only the verdicts in favor of the employee? Don't let people mislead you or scare you more than is warranted.

As for other types of "ADR"—early neutral evaluation, negotiation, conciliation, mediation—it is difficult for me to generalize. Negotiation is often a good idea. But I don't regard negotiation as an "alternative" to litigation. Nearly all litigation involves negotiation. In nearly all litigation, the judge or the rules of the court request, and sometimes even require, the parties to try to negotiate a settlement rather than go to trial. Much litigation is preceded by negotiation. That is, the employee's lawyer often writes a demand letter to the employer and tries to negotiate a settlement with the employer's lawyer first, before filing a lawsuit or demanding arbitration. Only if the negotiations fail does the plaintiff's lawyer file a lawsuit or demand arbitration.

Early neutral evaluation might be a good idea but it is often expensive and, if it doesn't result in a settlement, it often turns out to be a waste of money.

Mediation is like arbitration except that the mediator does not decide the case. The mediator tries to get the parties to reach a settlement. If they don't reach a settlement, they will probably either litigate or arbitrate, which often means the money you paid the mediator was a waste. Furthermore, an employer's eagerness to mediate can be interpreted by an employee as a sign of the employer's weakness. An employer who appears eager to mediate might be seen as an employer afraid to go to court. Why is the employer afraid to go to court? The employee might deduce that the employer likely violated the discrimination law. The employee will therefore demand more money from the employer to settle the case. Mediation is often a good idea, and it can be done in the course of, not just in lieu of, litigation or arbitration. It might help reach a settlement and thus obviate the need for a trial. Mediation is mandatory in some cases in some states.

I think employers should be willing to mediate, but when I represent employers who insist they did not violate the discrimination laws, I rarely, if ever, recommend that the employer initiate (that is, be the first to suggest) mediation in an employment discrimination lawsuit or arbitration. If the employee, judge, or arbitrator is the first to suggest mediation, I usually recommend to the employer to give mediation a try.

How about a multi-layered grievance system, so that an employee must first go through the hierarchy of the company and try to persuade the hierarchy to reverse the termination decision (if the employee was terminated), before filing suit or requesting arbitration? How about alternative fee agreements with lawyers, so that the company's law firm does not charge the company by the hour but rather by the result in the case or some combination of the result and the number of hours the lawyer worked on the case? I have my thoughts on these subjects but we are getting too far removed from the main subject of this book. The main subject of this book is faith-based human resource management.

Don't Lie to an Employee About Why You are Disciplining or Terminating Him

If you terminate an employee—that is, fire, lay off, or other situation in which an employee involuntarily is terminated from employment with your company or organization—don't lie to the employee about why you are terminating the employee. This does not mean that you must tell an employee all the reasons you are terminating him. Maybe you should tell him some of the reasons. In any event, don't tell him a lie. You can be vague; you don't have to explain things in detail. But don't tell a lie. If you terminate an employee who is black, female, older, disabled, gay, or in some other category of discrimination discussed in this book, and you lie to that employee about why you are terminating her, she can use that lie against you in an effort to prove that your real reason for firing her was her race, sex, age, disability, or other category of discrimination. A judge or jury might deem your lie to be a pretext—a lie you told in order to cover up your real reason for terminating the employee. A judge or jury might assume that your real reason for terminating the employee was that you don't like blacks, women, older workers, disabled workers, gays, or whatever classification that employee is in.

Let me illustrate. Suppose you fire an older worker because you think he is not intelligent enough for the job. You have a very intelligent young job applicant that you want to replace the older worker with. In your termination meeting with the older worker you try to be nice and you say, "We're sorry, but we're downsizing, so we have to let you go." After you terminate the older worker, you hire the young job applicant to perform that job. The older worker might sue you for age discrimination and have a pretty good case. Why? Because you lied to him. You were not downsizing. You replaced him with a new hire. This lie can be used in an effort to prove that your real reason for terminating him was his age. Does the law require you to be blunt and say, "You're fired because you're not intelligent enough for the job"? No, you are not required to say that. But don't tell him a lie. You can say, "We're not satisfied with your job performance" (if that is true). You can say, "We need someone who will produce more" (if that is true). You can say, "We need someone who is better with computers and

141

spreadsheets" (if that is true). There are other things you can say (if they are true). You can be vague. You can be tactful. Maybe, depending on circumstances, you don't have to give any reason at all. But don't lie.

Being truthful with the employee is usually the best strategy unless the truth is that you are discriminating against the employee because of his race, ethnicity, sex, age, or other protected classification. So, first know the truth yourself. Ask yourself, "Am I influenced in any way by the employee's race, ethnicity, sex, age, or other protected classification?" Put another way, "Am I doing anything illegal?" If your answer to these questions is no, you can probably fire the employee. If and when you fire the employee, tell the employee a true reason you are firing him. You do not necessarily have to tell him all the reasons you are firing him. You can tell him some of the reasons. Whatever you tell him, don't lie to him. You can probably guess which biblical passage I have in mind for this. I'm not certain this passage is always, 100% of the time, the best human resource management policy, but I think it is the best more often than not: "And you shall know the truth, and the truth shall make you free." John 8:32. First, know the truth yourself. Decide whether it is legal and wise for you to do what you want to do. Then, if you do it and announce it to the employee, tell the employee the truth or as much of the truth as is appropriate.

An employer should not lie to an employee about any adverse employment decision. Don't lie to an employee about why you are demoting him, cutting his pay, reducing his hours, transferring him to a less desirable location, laying him off, or making any other employment decision that will displease him. If he sues you, he can use the lie against you in an effort to prove that your real reason for taking such action was his race, sex, age, or other category of discrimination. You can be tactful, but don't lie.

Post All Required Notices and Undergo Any Required Training

Federal and state employment laws require employers to display certain posters telling employees what their rights are. Make sure you display all such posters—properly. Failure to display them properly can be used against you in court.

Chapter 11

Some Tips to Increase Profits and Wages

According to syndicated career-advice columnist Joyce Lain Kennedy, most layoff decisions, and I assume she would include most termination decisions, are based on "who earns their keep and who doesn't." "The key determinant of who survives layoffs is each employee's input to profit potential, based on his or her previous impact on bottom-line issues," she says in an article entitled "Who's Afraid of Layoffs?", http://www.sunfeatures.com/columns/2011/09-21-11.html (last visited Jan. 9, 2018). Some employers violate the discrimination laws, she observes, but most employers genuinely try to base their decisions on "who earns their keep and who doesn't," not on race, sex, age, and other discriminatory factors.

A layoff decision based on "who earns their keep and who doesn't" is acceptable, according to the Bible. "He who sows sparingly will also reap sparingly; and he who sows bountifully will also reap bountifully" (2 Corinthians 9:6). So it is difficult to criticize employers for basing decisions on "the bottom line." The bottom line should not be their only consideration, of course. Employers should also consider the economic and ecological effects of their operations and the good of all persons involved (Catechism, paragraph 2432). But basing decisions on the bottom line is good in this sense: It means, hopefully, that the employer is not basing decisions on race, sex, age, or other discriminatory factors.

The most important "color" in the workplace is not black or white. It is "green." "Green" can mean money, or it can mean environmentally friendly. Either way, "green" is the most important color in the workplace. Your decisions should be based on the economic, and hopefully also the ecological, "bottom line," not on an employee's race, sex, age, ethnicity, or other discriminatory category.

An important component of your bottom line is payroll. Your company or organization must pay wages that are high enough to comply with state and federal laws, such as the Fair Labor Standards Act. There is a minimum wage. You cannot pay an employee less than the minimum wage unless the law allows you to. In addition, many employees are entitled to premium pay—at least 1.5 times their regular rate of pay—for hours they work in excess of 40 in a week. A biblical passage the FLSA brings to mind is when Jesus said, "Come unto me, all ye that labor and are heavy laden, and I will give you rest" (Matthew 11:28). Hardworking employees deserve adequate rest. The FLSA encourages employers to provide rest. It does so by requiring employers to pay most (not all, but most) employees "time-and-a-half" for any hours worked in excess of 40 in a week. It encourages employers to hire additional employees rather than overwork current employees. This spreads employment to people who are unemployed or underemployed.

Perhaps the best tip we can give employees to prevent discrimination in the workplace is to be the best employee you can be. The best employees are discriminated against far less than the mediocre employees are. Most employers don't want to offend or lose the best employees. They want to keep the best employees. Most employers really do care more about "green" than any other color.

Then again, caring too much about "green" can lead to trouble, too. The Bible disapproves of employers who earn huge profits from their employees' labor and live extravagantly but pay their employees poorly. That is not discrimination, however. It is greed. Greed is relevant to discrimination in this respect: Employers who live extravagantly are probably more likely to get sued for discrimination (not necessarily more likely to lose a discrimination suit, but more likely to get sued in the first place) than employers who don't. Many fired employees sue their employer not because they really believe their employer discriminated or otherwise violated the law but because they are angry and need money. They resent their employer's living extravagantly off the employee's labor and then dumping the employee onto the street. They want the employer to "share the wealth" more by paying the employee a settlement package or jury verdict. An employee who is earning a modest hourly wage and gets fired might sue the employer for discrimination and seek hundreds of thousands of dollars in damages. The employer will react as though the employee is some kind of thief trying to steal the employer's money.

The employee has no right to the money, argues the employer. But even if the employer is correct—even if the suit has no basis—the employer should recall the words of Jesus: "Do not lay up for yourselves treasures on earth, where moths and rust destroy and where thieves break in and steal" (Matthew 6:19). The more "treasure" the employer shows off, the more likely a disgruntled employee will try to "steal" it.

The employer will no doubt respond, "I earned my money honestly. I worked very hard for it, harder than most of my employees work. I took risks they did not take. I am entitled to live in luxury. My employees are not entitled to sue me unless I violated their rights. I have not violated their rights." Even if these employers are correct, I surmise (perhaps I'm mistaken) that if they lived more modestly, fewer employees would sue them. Much litigation in this country is simply an effort by poor and modest-means people to redistribute wealth by suing the rich. Employers, especially large employers, are often referred to as "deep pockets" in legal jargon. Poor and modest-means plaintiffs try to get their hands into the "deep pockets" of employers, insurance companies, the government, and other "deep pockets." So, one way employers can reduce the number of discrimination lawsuits is to live less extravagantly.

Of course, not every employer is rich and not every employer lives extravagantly. Employees should keep that in mind. Employees who feel like victims of discrimination should realize that employers often feel like victims, too. Employers feel like victims when employees do not try their hardest; when employees make mistakes that cause their employers to lose money and customers; when employees fail, for whatever reason, to generate enough revenue for their employer to pay their salaries; when poorly-performing employees erroneously believe they are victims of discrimination; and when employees learn their employer's business and then go to work for a competitor. Employees should keep in mind that eight out of ten businesses fail. These failures cause financial losses, and sometimes great financial hardship, to the owners. Even employers who accumulate some wealth sometimes lose that wealth quickly when times get tough. Paying employees during hard times can drain hundreds of thousands of dollars, or even millions of dollars, from an employer in a short period of time.

That is why most employees never try to become employers themselves. They know it is financially risky. They know eight out of ten fail. It is a good thing that some people try to be employers, because if no one did, there would be no jobs.

Chapter 12

Saints and Jobs

The financial risks of being an employer—particularly the risk of starting a business and hiring an employee to begin with—are no doubt what St. Peter had in mind when he said, "Servants, be submissive to your masters with all fear, not only to the good and gentle, but also to the harsh" (1 Peter 2:18). Even a harsh employer deserves credit for one thing: He or she gives people jobs. He or she provides people with a living. If the people who complain about "harsh" employers had to meet a payroll themselves, they would probably be harsh, too.

Most employers are not "saints." But then, most "saints" are not employers. Most "saints"—nice people such as schoolteachers, social workers, nurses, the clergy, and others who go around doing good deeds and are never accused of being "harsh" or "cheap" like employers are—do not provide many jobs. They do not pay people much money. People need money to buy food, clothing, shelter, and the other necessities and amenities of life. They receive most of that money from "harsh," "cheap" employers, not from "saints." That is basically what St. Peter was telling us: We need "saints," but we also need employers. It is difficult to be both.

St. Paul, too, recognized the need for employers and jobs. Paul said to Titus, "Exhort servants to be obedient to their own masters, to be well pleasing in all things, not answering back, not pilfering, but showing all good fidelity" (Titus 2:9-10). Paul wanted to reward people for taking the risks necessary to become employers and provide jobs. Paul did not want to reward employers too much, however. He did not want power to go to their heads. So he admonished them, "Masters, give your servants what is just and fair, knowing that you also have a Master in heaven" (Colossians 4:1).

So it all boils down to this: Employers should be fair to their employees, and their employees should appreciate having jobs.

About the Author

David A. Robinson was born in Springfield, Massachusetts, in 1953. In 1974 he earned a B.A. in economics from George Washington University in Washington, DC. In 1977 he earned a J.D. from Washington University in St. Louis. He returned to Springfield, was admitted to the Massachusetts bar, and practiced law in Springfield from 1977 to 2008.

David did not get married until he was 50 years old, in 2003. He and his wife decided to live in the New Haven, CT, area, where she is from, rather than in Massachusetts. He gradually closed his Massachusetts law practice, was admitted to the Connecticut Bar in 2006, and taught business law, business ethics, and human resource management at the University of New Haven from 2005 to 2014. He now practices employment law in Connecticut.

Made in the USA
Las Vegas, NV
29 December 2021

39764106R00094